NYLLFF

We hope you enjoy this book. Please return or
renew it by the due date. You can renew it at
www.norfolk.gov.uk/libraries or by using our free
library app. Otherwise you can phone
0344 800 8020 - please have your library card and
PIN ready. You can sign up for email reminders too.

NORFOLK COUNTY COUNCIL
LIBRARY AND INFORMATION SERVICE

PRISONER OF THE SAMURAI

PRISONER OF THE SAMURAI

Surviving the Sinking of the U.S.S. *Houston* and the Death Railway

Rosalie H. Smith R N
as related by James Wallace Gee, Private, USMC

CASEMATE

Philadelphia & Oxford

Published in the United States of America and Great Britain in 2018 by
CASEMATE PUBLISHERS
1950 Lawrence Road, Havertown, PA 19083, USA
and
The Old Music Hall, 106–108 Cowley Road, Oxford OX4 1JE, UK

Hardcover Edition: ISBN 978-1-61200-597-3
Digital Edition: ISBN 978-1-61200-598-0 (epub)

A CIP record for this book is available from the Library of Congress and the British Library

Printed and bound in the United States of America

For a complete list of Casemate titles, please contact:

CASEMATE PUBLISHERS (US)
Telephone (610) 853-9131
Fax (610) 853-9146
Email: casemate@casematepublishers.com
www.casematepublishers.com

CASEMATE PUBLISHERS (UK)
Telephone (01865) 241249
Fax (01865) 794449
Email: casemate-uk@casematepublishers.co.uk
www.casematepublishers.co.uk

To the valiant crew of the U.S.S. *Houston*

Contents

Editor's Note

During World War II, Lieutenant Rosalie Hamric was an R.N., serving as Charge Nurse in the Psychiatric Ward of the Guantanamo Bay Naval Hospital. At the end of the war, a group of liberated P.O.Ws from Southeast Asia (survivors of the sinking of the U.S.S. *Houston*) was sent to this ward for treatment. Many were encouraged to write down their experiences as part of their therapy and for the sake of all those who did not make it to Guantanamo.* One, James Gee, PFC, USMC did a particularly detailed job. During the course of his treatment, he and other POWs shared many of these experiences with Rosalie, who wove them into this account. After her death, the manuscript was found in an attic and, although its conclusions were made at the time of the Viet Nam War, the sentiments are just as timely in our day of "wars and rumors of wars." This is especially true in light of the fact that 2017 is the 75th anniversary of the sinking of the *Houston*.

Special appreciation must be given to Craig Smith, "he of the eagle eye," whose contributions are immeasurable in making this book clear, concise and accurate; to Brad Gee, who filled in so many gaps and provided photos of his father, and to the survivors of the sinking of the *Houston*, whose story of courage and tenacity this is.

—Allyson Smith

---

* Some names have been changed.

CHAPTER I

The Honor

It was a hot, still afternoon in Austin, Texas. On the University grounds, not a leaf, twig or blade of grass moved. The heat was oppressive and enervating; it dulled the mind and weighted the spirit. From outside the open classroom window the sleepy-sounding buzz of bees floated into the room to compete with our English instructor's reading of Byron. I had long planned a political career. While at the university I had made campaign speeches for one of the candidates for Lieutenant Governor. My father and Governor O'Daniels had been friends since childhood and I could remember many good times in the Governor's Mansion. Both the Governor and my father had encouraged my political ambitions. As a young fellow, I had informed them that I intended to be Governor of Texas one day.

Many of my classmates at the University of Texas had joined the Canadian Air Force, and had already seen much action in the European theater. Our sphere of operations was dead. Despite a constant threat, no war was in evidence. My immediate problem was to teach my ambition to conform to the facts. I had enjoyed Veblen, Montaigne, Kipling, Geography and a host of other somewhat more frivolous pursuits on campus, but, as Hitler's panzers rolled over country after country, it seemed abundantly evident that the United States would be involved at any moment. Several friends and I did manage to finish our second semester, but when June, 1940 arrived, we joined the U.S. Marine Corps.

There were approximately 1,000 men in the Asiatic Fleet. Out of this number, four sailors and three marines had been notified that they were to complete certain courses under a wardroom class with Marine Captain Ramsey. I was one of these. We were recruits for the Naval Academy at Annapolis.

I had been studying hard for three months. Then, we got our ship assignment: we were to have the honor of serving aboard the U.S.S. *Houston.*

She was big, very big and she'd become famous; from Europe to Texas, through the Panama Canal and out to Honolulu. On February 22, 1931* the U.S.S. *Houston* joined the Asiatic Fleet in Manila, Philippine Islands, and assumed her role as flagship, hoisting the flag of Admiral Charles McVay, Jr. The flooding of the Yangtze River in September of that year necessitated the use of the *Houston* for rescue work; this flood was one of the most devastating in the history of that most renowned river. The *Houston* went up the river for about 600 miles, to the city of Hankow, returning to Shanghai on October 5, 1931.

During a routine overhaul in the Cavite Naval Yard, Philippine Islands, on the night of January 31, 1932, the *Houston* was given orders to proceed immediately to Shanghai. Hostilities had broken out between Japan and China. American lives and interests were endangered. Within two hours she sailed with 250 marines to augment the 4th Marine Regiment stationed in Shanghai. Although the weather conditions were rough, the ship broke all existing records, making the trip in 47 hours.

The *Houston* left Manila on March 13, 1933, on a goodwill tour through the southern Philippines, visiting Iloilo, Cebu, Davao, Dumanquilas Bay and Zamboango. On May 29, 1933 she made a goodwill tour to Japan, visiting Yokohama and Kobe, returning to Tsingtao, China by way of the Japanese Inland Sea. On November 17, 1933, she was relieved by the U.S.S. *Augusta,* and departed from Shanghai for San Francisco, visiting Yokohama en route. She was overhauled in the Puget Sound Navy yard, joining a scouting force of the U.S. fleet in Long Beach, California and departed with the fleet for Atlantic ports.

While at Annapolis, Maryland, on July 1, 1934, President Roosevelt came aboard the *Houston,* for a cruise of 11,783 miles. The party accompanying him consisted of his two sons, John, and Franklin Delano,

---

* Dates are stateside.

Jr., his naval aide, Captain Wilson Brown, Mr. R. Forster, Executive Clerk, Commander Ross T. McIntyre (MC) U.S.N. plus R. Jervis and G. Gennerich of the U.S. Secret Service. The destroyers U.S.S. *Gilmer* and U.S.S. *Williamson* transported the press representatives, and acted as escorts until the *Houston* arrived at the Canal Zone where they were relieved by the cruiser U.S.S. *New Orleans*.

First stop was laid off Long Island, in the upper Bahamas, on July 4, while the President enjoyed a day of fishing. The first port of call was Cape Hatien, Haiti, where the President exchanged calls with President Vicente of Haiti. The next port was Mayguez, Puerto Rico, where the President and his entourage disembarked and motored across the island to rejoin the ships at San Juan. They proceeded to St. Thomas and St. Croix, Virgin Islands, and to Cartagena, Colombia, South America, where the President undertook a goodwill visit. The *Houston* stopped at Cristobal, Canal Zone, to allow the Hon. Mr. Dern, Secretary of War, to come aboard.

During passage through the canal, the military defense force was presented to the President and the Secretary of War, and was unanimously acclaimed for the excellent appearance of both personnel and fighting equipment. At Balboa, the President received on board the President of Balboa along with other prominent personages. At Cocos Island, famous as a buccaneer haunt, the President had another day of fishing. The *Houston* proceeded toward the next stop, and when approximately 1,000 miles from land, two land-based aircraft appeared, followed by the enormous dirigible U.S.S. *Macon*.

Newspapers and mail, which were only 24 hours old, were delivered to the President. The planes were then drawn up into an enclosure in the *Macon*, and the giant dirigible returned to her base near San Francisco. A brief visit to Clipperton Island was made, and the next stop was Hilo territory of Hawaii where 60,000 people lined the docks to catch a glimpse of the famous man aboard. Two days were spent in Hawaii before proceeding Portland, Oregon where the President disembarked.

After a two-week overhaul in San Diego, California, the *Houston* got under way for Norfolk and New York, joined the fleet and visited its natal city. Here it engaged in fleet maneuvers, returning to the Pacific coast in November for gunnery practice and engineering tests.

On May 16, 1935, in San Diego, Henry L. Roosevelt, Assistant Secretary of the Navy, came aboard and his flag was hoisted. He remained aboard during a voyage to Hawaii, and returned to San Pedro, California on June 1, where he disembarked and departed for Washington, D.C.

The *Houston* rejoined the fleet in San Diego for Navy Week, in connection with the Pacific Exposition, there in progress. In one year she had steamed 37,326 miles.

CHAPTER 2

"My Mama Nice Virgin"

Soon after we boarded, the *Houston* got underway for Hawaii. We spent the next two days standing watches and receiving instructions in the use of firearms, both small and the larger guns. At the end of the second day, we ran into rough weather and many of us were too sick to care about danger, war or how to fire a gun.

"That bastard Hitler has poisoned us!" moaned Tom O'Neil, a tall, handsome PFC from Dallas who was returning from yet another trip to the head. Tom was the self-appointed lady-killer of our group. "You've heard of this psychological warfare, haven't you?" he asked.

"Better call the corpsman, somebody. O'Neil's losing it," diagnosed Marv, who himself was beginning to recover from his nausea.

"What a bunch of Sad Sacks you guys are. A couple of big waves and yer flat on yer asses. What did you think you were getting into, Sunday School?" sneered Chuck Satterlee.

Chuck bore a startling resemblance to Wallace Beery—or at least what I thought Wallace Beery must have looked like at the age of thirty. He was ten years older than most of us and had risen to the rank of corporal … twice. He had been broken twice—once for clouting a chief and once for landing a haymaker on a bosun's jaw. He was now a PFC and had to suffer the indignity of standing watch with the rest of us. His temper was whispered to be the kind you read about in the medical journals or on the front page of a tabloid. We all knew he usually got upset after a letter from his wife Gertrude.

"Why did you join the service, Chuck?" I asked, trying to hear his answer over the thumping of my nervous heart.

"Well, I joined to get away from Gertrude. I drank too many zombies and woke up married to one. I thought it might make me feel better if I could run a bayonet through some enemy guts."

"Ooooh!" moaned O'Neil and dashed for the head again. Chuck seemed to be the only one who felt like talking and his choice of topics did little to calm our already queasy stomachs.

"If I'd never seen a broad, I'd be a happy man. I never intended to get married. You guys are different. You got nice homes and families and you shoulda waited to be drafted. You get sent to the Far East where it's warm, so that's OK, but who says you won't draw duty around Greenland or somewhere where it's colder 'n a witch's tits?"

"If you'd heard that band playin' in Dallas that day, you'd have joined, too!" said Marv, drawing his pale eyebrows together.

"Yeah, that's all it means to you kids!" Chuck retorted. "I think you'd be a helluva lot wiser if you woke up some morning with a leg shot off or an eye gone or maybe two. That's what's gonna happen to some of us. We're gonna have a war and damn soon It's probably already started."

"I wouldn't worry too much about us, Chuck," put in Strong. Gordon Strong was a large, cheerful, redhead whose hair was just beginning to recede near the temples. He was that rare sort of man who never says anything derogatory about anyone, sees no ulterior motive in anyone, is full of enthusiasm for life in general and goes out of his way to help others. He was deeply religious but made no public display of his faith other than in his behavior. At the same time, he was one of the boys and no one ever called him goody-goody. Needless to say, he was one of the most popular men on the ship. I felt lucky that he usually spent his liberties with me when we were not on opposite watches.

"We couldn't," Strong continued, "concentrate on school work, Chuck, with a war coming. A fellow has to do his part and get it over with. None of us wanted this war, but since we're getting it anyway, we have to be realistic. We can't just stick our heads in the sand. I'm not worried about what's going to happen to us. All of us'll get back who really believe we'll get back. It's as simple as that."

"That's just too damn simple for me to get through my damn skull," Chuck snorted. "Why ask for trouble?"

We began to get our sea legs and, by the time we docked in Pearl Harbor, we were ready for liberty. Strong and I walked the streets, frankly rubber-necking. This land was so very different from Texas and we wanted to make sure we saw as much of it as possible.

We learned that there were three main forms of entertainment for servicemen and I list them in order of their popularity: 1) Visiting the local houses of prostitution, 2) Guzzling beer in the local slop chute, 3) Sightseeing.

While we were making like tourists, we saw a long line of men in front of a large, rather dilapidated house. It was obviously not a beer hall, but from the number of men queued up in front of it, I knew it must contain some attraction.

"Look at that one, Gordon," I exclaimed "Must be some kind of museum. Let's go take a look."

We walked over to the end of the line. Before we could ask any questions, a swarthy man wearing a brightly flowered sarong sidled up to me and asked: "Whicha your girl?"

"No girl," I replied, beginning to catch on.

"Three dollah. Stand in line, please," said the pimp in a rapid sing-song and moved on, looking for more customers.

Strong and I started to leave, but the little pimp came back. "No long wait," he assured us. "Line movah very fast. Three dollah, only."

"We've had a rough crossing, mate," said Strong, giving him a big smile.

At this time a fat army major, bearing a huge sack of groceries took his place at the end of the line. He seemed completely nonchalant as he settled his bag of groceries on one hip for the wait. Giving him credit for his courage, we pushed on toward the beach.

Waikiki Beach surpassed my wildest expectations, coming from north of the Dallas area where a lakeshore was as much as you could expect. The shining beach, with it backdrop of royal palms, rustling softy in the harbor breeze framed the most amazing turquoise water I had ever seen.

We were coming out of the water after taking a dip when Tom O'Neil came walking along the beach. A large simulated blonde was swinging from one arm and a brunette followed close behind.

He introduced us to the girls and we had sandwiches and sodas at a seaside stand. For the next three afternoons we swam with them, tried surfboards and achieved some decent tans on the sugar-like sands.

After several days of seeing most every tourist attraction we could find on what proved (in comparison to Texas' endless expanse) a rather small area, I was having a serious bout of homesickness. I wondered why I had not married my best girl, Alicia, despite the objection of both our parents, who felt we were too young. Now, she would be prey to who knows how many cowboys without me there to stake my claim.

After ten days, the *Houston* upped anchor and headed for Guam. The feeling of depression persisted and I had the miserable feeling that I would never see Alicia again or the islands of Hawaii. I had had no real experience with war, yet I felt I had heard enough of it. It was the chief topic of conversation, constantly on our minds and every discussion of our futures was prefaced with a large IF.

Thankfully, we had a calm sea to Guam and arrived right after lunchtime, one day after the visit of a heavy typhoon. The storm had spent itself and large, white cumulus clouds drifted lazily across a sky of intense blue. Everything had been lashed down to prevent its being blown away.

The sun was shining and I caught a monstrous view of tall, dark brown cliffs, vegetation turned a dark brown by the saltwater spray and one, lone white hotel, which I later learned was the Pan-American.

My first impression of Guam was a disappointing one, but as we climbed aboard the liberty boat and motored through the impossibly clear sea toward the beautiful white coral beaches, my opinion improved. This, too, was very different from Texas, which, for most of us, still served as the yardstick by which we measured everything from topography to girls.

We were given four hours' liberty. Strong, Jones and I were systematically investigating the curio shops which were stocked with polished seashells, pictures and belts made from beads, shells and ox-hide, when O'Neil burst into to one of the shops. He tore off his overseas cap and slammed it against the top of a table, obviously scorched about something.

"What's the matter with you?" asked Gordon.

O'Neil drew a deep breath and let it out slowly, his face registering disgust and frustration. "Those dirty sonsabitches have locked up all the women on this blasted island!" he complained bitterly.

"How sad," responded Jones, in mock sympathy, "Wanna borrow my cryin' towel?"

"Go see the chaplain," I suggested. "Tell him the MPs have locked up all the prostitutes."

"Just give me some poison," O'Neil said, sadly. Suddenly his face lit up with inspiration and he bestowed upon us the full benefit of his flashing white smile. "Let's go get some tuba! It's a native drink that they make out of coconut milk. Pure poison!"

I remembered O'Neil's description of the drink two hours later when we were boarding the liberty boat to return to the ship.

Many of the crew members were groggy from the fermented coconut milk and took some tricky management by their friends. O'Neil was one of those who had overestimated his tolerance for the stuff. He kept insulting a burly sailor who returned the insults with alacrity and considerable warmth. Both men had had too much. We managed to keep them separated until, half way to the *Houston*, a heavy swell forced all of us to grab for support. O'Neil lunged for the sailor before the boat righted itself, the sailor grappled with him and when a second swell arrived both men fell overboard. We fished them out and O'Neil's black curls were straighter than a cat that had fallen in a horse trough.

This liberty did little for any of us except furnish a change of scene and of pace. I was not sorry when the *Houston* pulled out and headed for the Philippines. Morale on the ship was very high en route, however. We wrestled, boxed, sang and viewed movies. The weather was outstanding. A huge, golden moon hung in a cloudless sky, a gentle breeze played across the deck and there was the constant sound of waves lapping the ship's sides as she rolled.

Marv Jones, who had refrained from practical jokes since the third day aboard, grew restless. We had a sailor aboard whom we called The Kid who was a terrific boxer. He later became champion of the Asiatic Fleet.

It was not surprising that it was sometimes difficult to find challengers for him. Jones was very helpful. Without my knowledge, he saw the

Rec. Officer and told him I wanted to box the sailor. Ten minutes later, while I was in Ship's Service buying razor blades, Strong, Chuck and O'Neil burst through the door and began slapping me on the back in a state of considerable excitement.

"Hey! Take it easy! What's cooking" I asked, not having an inkling of what I had done to deserve this commendation.

"You've decided to challenge The Kid, eh? Man, what a nerve you've got!" exclaimed O'Neil while he ran the fingers of his right hand back and forth through his short, curly mop.

I must have had a blank expression on my face, because Chuck began tugging at his cauliflower ear in a puzzled way. "I'm beginning to smell a whale-sized rat in this deal. That buzzard Jones has been up to one of his half-assed practical jokes again," he growled.

He had, indeed. We went to see the Rec. Officer on the double. I agreed to fight The Kid, but we arranged to make the joke backfire on Jones.

On the night of the fight, Jones was to wrestle a sailor. When he came out in the wrestling trunks, the corporal called him over.

"By the way, Jones," he said, hurriedly, "we have a shortage of athletic equipment just now. Just keep those shorts on for your bout with The Kid."

Jones's mouth fell open as though his jawbone had suddenly turned to jelly and he started to say something to the corporal in protest, but the only thing that came out was: "But ... but ... but..."

At this point, the Rec. Officer came up and told him to get into the ring and stop holding up the show.

Marv was not a professional wrestler, but he had done some collegiate wrestling and usually gave a good performance. Tonight, however, his mind was not on his work. The sailor opposing him had no difficulty pinning his shoulders to the mat and did this twice before I went to change into trunks. When I returned, the bout was over and Marv had lost.

The Kid stepped into the ring and the corporal, looking at his clipboard, started toward the tow-headed, white-faced Jones. Strong and O'Neil were standing up to make a screen for me.

With furrowed eyebrows, Jones began to rub his solar plexus. "I don't feel so good. That last throw shook me up!"

"Seems like I remember hearing you saying that all the guys on this ship are chicken," put in Chuck. "Do you remember saying that, Marvin?" Jones looked desperately unhappy and, thinking the joke had gone far enough, I got into the ring.

I fought The Kid and lived. After the bout Marv was sulking. It seems that a lot of practical jokers can dish it out but they can't take it. The guys started calling him "The Promoter" and Chuck asked him to get a bout for him with Joe Louis as soon as the *Houston* hit the States.

Jones, flushing to his pale roots, peered at Chuck and said, softly, "You dirty bastards!"

It was several days before Marv could talk rationally about the incident.

Ten days from Guam, cruising at 15 knots, we arrived in Manila Bay on November 18. I had heard a great deal about this "Pearl of the Orient" and I was intensely interested in seeing as much of the Philippines as I could while I was still alive to do it.

I had just finished reading a letter from my sister, Jackie. It was typical of the attitude my sisters were taking. After the usual news about home-town events and people, she finished with the naïve but sisterly request that I "Please go see the captain and get a transfer. There's really going to be a war and you might get killed!"

As we steamed into the bay, the Fortress of Corregidor came into view on our starboard bow, followed by innumerable small islands. Some of these were covered with dense, green tropical vegetation, while others appeared completely barren and quite desolate.

The first structures I saw were the tall radio towers then the white, beautiful city nestling among green and brown palms. The sandy shore-line cut the blue water and then a row of white office buildings appeared. Beyond this, beautiful Spanish-style homes and churches, interspersed with brown patches of Nipa huts made of grass matting and bamboo with thatched bamboo roofs.

We anchored in the bay and port watch was given liberty. We always wondered if each liberty might be our last. Strong, O'Neil and I went ashore. When the liberty boat landed, hordes of small, brown Filipinos swarmed us.

"Shine, Joe? Want a paper, Joe? Gimme a nickel, Joe!"

We bought papers, had shines and scattered change among the throng. One small urchin continued to follow us. Strong gave him a nickel, but he kept mumbling until O'Neil stopped, squatted before the small boy, flashed his famous grin and asked, "Whatsa matter, kid? What'd ya expect, egg in your beer?"

"Wanna ... see my mama? She nice virgin!" the child replied.

"Keeerist!" declared O'Neil, "Get this kid! Pimpin' for his old lady!"

I was astounded. I almost asked the boy to repeat himself. My first reaction to Philippine night life was a feeling of disgust. Later, I realized how little I knew about the Orient.

Each of us gave the kid a dime and O'Neil told him to take the day off. Strong and I hired a horse-drawn *kalisa*, a cart, and made a tour of the city. O'Neil stopped in a joint where several sailors and marines from the ship were tying one on.

The streets were unbelievably congested with cars and *kalisas* and the sidewalk teemed with people of every nationality. We saw the old fortress which Admiral Dewey had bombarded at the time of his entrance into Manila Bay. The many years of exposure to salt spray and tropical storms had taken their toll, but it somehow remained ageless and indomitable.

After a visit to some curio shops where I bought presents for my family and Alicia, we visited the slums and native villages. Poor sanitation, substandard housing and unbelievable crowding made us realize that the term Pearl of the Orient was accurate only when seen from a distance.

On the following morning, November 19 at 1000 hours, the *Houston* became the flagship for the Asiatic Fleet. Admiral Hart came aboard and his flag was raised. The bands of both ships broke into "San Francisco, Here I come" and the U.S.S. *Augustus* got under way for the States.

Before our next liberty, O'Neil held a symposium on how to pick a prostitute.

"Better get a little horizontal refreshment while you can, fellahs, we might all be dead this time next week," he began. "Fifteen is a good age," he stated authoritatively, "because by that age they've had some experience, but, if they're lucky, they don't have the clap yet. Don't pick one who's just arrived from the provinces because she's too green. And don't pick one who's ready to go back, 'cause she'll be too baggy and loose. Steer clear of the kids with their old man and old lady doin' the dickering. They overcharge and they don't give a damn for the guy. They just want the dough. Make the deal with the gal herself then she'll fall for you and spend the money on you."

"Don't loan 'em any money, either" put in Chuck. "Some who are old and don't want to go back to the provinces just hang around the bars and streets hopin' for a handout. They can't cut the mustard anymore. One old gal grabbed hold of my sleeve and said, 'Hey, Yank! Loan me a buck 'til I can get on my back.'"

A number of the men on the *Houston* were infatuated with Estrelita, a movie star who had appeared in a number of jungle pictures. She had danced and sung in Singapore and India, and was now appearing at the best club in Manila. I accompanied John Sayre, a broad-shouldered, genial crooner from Missouri, to the club one night. John had met an attractive American girl who was a good friend of Estrelita's.

The three of us were sitting at a table talking when the band started playing very loudly and one of the most beautiful girls I have ever seen stepped into the spotlight.

She was tall with a creamy skin, enormous, luminous dark eyes, dark, silky hair curling about her shoulders, even features and a beautiful smile. I watched her, fascinated, and, when she began to sing, she sent me to the moon in a hurry. At first I thought it was the cocktail but, after her performance, she came and sat at our table.

"This is Estrelita," said John. I was thinking, as I acknowledged the introduction, that she had a face and figure to rival any Hollywood star. Estrelita close up was something even more amazing. I caught the faint fragrance of her perfume, gawked into the luminous eyes, felt my pulse pound and knew instantly that this creature embodied all the allure of the Far East.

"Shall we dance?" I asked huskily.

She nodded and as we reached the dance floor I swept her into my arms to the strains of "Green Eyes." This was something to write home about!

I attended church festivals, went to museums, libraries and parties with Estrelita. Throughout this time, the *Houston* was in and out of Manila on maneuvers. We were told over and over again that we could expect war at any time.

One night after a month of practice firing and general maneuvers, we were anchored in the harbor of Iloilo on the southeastern coast of Panay. I was standing the midnight watch as guard of the skipper. Except for the hum of the auxiliary engines and the buzz of mosquitoes as they dive-bombed every part of me that wasn't covered, the ship was quiet.

The mosquitoes in the Far East are larger than those in Texas. Chuck swore that four could carry off a horse. They look like grand-daddy long-legs. They land on your skin and, while you are deciding that a mosquito could never grow to that size, they bayonet you and take off.

In between swats, I was busy musing over a physics problem for the next wardroom class under Marine Captain Ramsey. Having been chosen from the fleet as a candidate for Annapolis, it was important that I did not waste this opportunity. Needless to say, the time spent on watch added to classes in math, geography, English and history left me little time for daydreaming.

I had never thought of myself as a career man in the service. It seemed like a fine thing—for someone else. I realized, however, that there was a great need for officers in wartime and, since I could not very well study law under the existing circumstances, I was pleased to be able to learn anything, and felt the honor keenly.

My mother had been delighted. Southern families in general have a high regard for Academy-trained men and, to her mind, the time spent negotiating the ladder from plebe to ensign was four years in which she could be relatively sure I *was* alive.

I felt that I had solved the physics problem and allowed my thoughts to drift as I paced back and forth in the hallway. In my mind's eye, I was already walking down the steps of the Naval Academy chapel, dodging the crossed swords of my classmates, a radiant Alicia clinging to my arm, when I heard staccato footsteps coming down the normally very quiet passageway. I stopped, prepared as usual for anything, not really expecting to use my mental or physical prowess, let alone my sidearm, but rather concerned that some dunderhead had the nerve to create a disturbance near the skipper's cabin at this hour.

"You awaken the captain, sonny," I was mentally telling my unknown visitor, "and I'll string you up to a green apple tree!" Just where I would find the necessary props did not concern me in the least at that moment. I only knew that Captain Rooks had apparently not been feeling well when he retired. He never went to bed before I came on watch, but read or studied late into the night. He was the most thoughtful and generally considerate officer I had ever encountered, frequently offering me a book that might help me with my proposed career as a line officer, or suggesting that I take a chair from his cabin on which to sit while doing my homework. I rarely complied, but I did appreciate the courtesy he showed me.

I looked at my watch. It was 0330 and not yet time for my relief. A radioman third class came into view. The moment I saw his face, my feeling of annoyance turned to one of concern. His general demeanor gave me the impression that he had just received a profound shock. He saluted. I returned the salute and took the piece of folded paper he handed me. Apparently noting the expression of inquiry on my face, he told me in a strained voice that a somewhat garbled message had been received. It was of the gravest importance that the skipper be awakened at once! Before I realized the full import of what he was saying, he had disappeared.

I did not waste time awakening Captain Rooks. While I saluted him in a most formal and military fashion, clicking the heels of my highly polished brown shoes, I kept thinking "This must be war! This must be it!" Yet there were always false alarms. Rumors on a ship spread faster than a sneeze through a screen door.

The skipper sat up in bed, looked quizzically at me then at his watch. Seeing the piece of paper in my hand, he was instantly alert and, taking it from me, perused it quickly. He appeared quite puzzled then worried and, finally, on rereading it for the third time, a look of incredulity swept his face. Pushing the blankets away, he swung his legs in one rapid motion over the side of the bed.

"This is bad, very bad!" he told me, his face taut and white with alarm beneath the yellow light. "I'll dress and go topside!"

He dressed rapidly and I accompanied him topside to the radio shack where he talked in short, clipped sentences to the officer on watch. In the 15 months since the *Houston* had left the States, I had never seen the skipper react in this fashion to any message I had given him. Both officers appeared to be not just angry, but outraged.

When they had finished their conversation, the captain turned and we retraced our steps to the cabin. At the door he turned, his brows knit, his eyes dark with alarm. "Stand by for something more definite," he said. "There will be other messages. I will not be sleeping."

As I closed the cabin door on him, Homer Miller, a tall, blond marine from Minnesota, appeared to. relieve me. I briefed him on what had transpired and went topside and stood looking over the rail into the dark water below. Until I knew more, sleep was out of the question. We must be at war. I thought of home and my pre-Law studies, somewhat impulsively abandoned to go to sea to fight a war that had, until now, failed to materialize. Had it begun, or was it another false alarm? I went down below to talk to the guys.

The news of war was not unexpected, but we had anticipated it too long. The idea of the lowly Jap striking at the heart of the Pacific Fleet was incomprehensible. We had trouble realizing its significance. The concrete reality of war suddenly replacing a dim abstraction of a future war presented problems which we had not anticipated.

"I hope this isn't what I think it is," said Marv, his blue eyes clouding with pre-occupation. They have too many people on their little islands and they've gotta do something. I don't say they are justified in attacking us; I'm flabbergasted that they did, but overpopulation is a real problem for them."

"I know just how to fix that!" Chuck snorted. "I've got just the thing. I got me one of these here Kris knives, the kind the Moros use. I'll be glad to remove the parts that are making them rowdy, if you know what I mean!"

"They need education, not emasculation. A little birth control might help, too," from Chaplain Gray, who arrived in time to hear Chuck's solution. "I think it would be wise not to underestimate them. They have never been defeated."

"You mean this'll be the first time," said Gordon, simply. "They have a new experience coming to them!"

"That's the attitude we must take, of course. We must have faith. Faith is power, men. All human exertion is given meaning by faith. In a more elevated sense it is a spiritual force in and of itself. I strongly urge you men to think about that. Have you written to your mothers and fathers?"

I was glad that I had. I was thinking quite nostalgically of how it had been 15 months since I had seen the wide plains of our Texas ranch when Homer Miller delivered to Captain Rooks the message of the bombing of Pearl Harbor. It was 0500.

Since it was an hour before sunrise, the skipper gave an order not to arouse the sleeping crew. Thirty minutes later, general quarters was sounded and the official news was announced to the crew. Condition X-Ray was set, steel plates were welded over the portholes and the *Houston* was ready for action.

Although all of us had expected war for many months, the concrete reality was many times more startling than any dim abstraction of a possible future war. The news left us in a mild state of shock. Our first thoughts were of families and friends. Then, the ship buzzed with conjecture and every man's version of what should be done to the Japs in retaliation. Finally, after the first indignation had died down somewhat, the conversations became more serious and hearts were heavier

At my first opportunity, I wrote my parents and Alicia, telling them not to worry. "The enemy," I assured them, "will never molest the Flagship. I could not be safer."

Orders were to stand by at Iloilo until Admiral Glassford, who had been in charge of the Yangtze River Patrol, could come aboard and take command of the Asiatic Fleet. At approximately 1730, he arrived by plane, coming to the *Houston* by whaleboat. At 1800, the fleet was underway. Temporary headquarters of the Allied Naval Forces had been established at Java, under the command of Admiral Thomas C. Hart. The fleet was to start convoying Allied ships between the Philippines, Java and Australia. Our immediate destination was Soerbaja, Java.

We anticipated trouble at any second. The Japanese had already bombed the Philippines; Manila had been hit, and Iloilo could be their next target. Our ships carried a valuable cargo of gold, ammunition, and aviation fuel. I was given a new assignment as rammerman on the

No. 7 5-inch gun. We headed out into the Guimaras Strait toward the Sulu Sea. There was no evidence of the enemy, but, after an hour and a half, when Iloilo had dropped below the horizon, we heard a series of loud explosions and knew that either the enemy or local saboteurs had blown up the oil reserves.

The *Houston* was accompanied by the *Marblehead*, a light cruiser, the supply ships, 13 destroyers and the *Langley*, an old aircraft carrier. One of the destroyers, the *Paul Jones*, was assigned advanced guard duty. We steamed along peacefully through the Sulu Sea without incident. This continued from the night of the 8th through the 10th.

I was standing alternate watches behind the gun and in the 5-inch ammunition magazine, two decks below the waterline. To be honest, I have to admit that, of the two assignments, I preferred the topside one where my position behind the gun allowed me a ringside seat. We were all spoiling for an encounter with the Japs.

Our progress was relatively slow, because we were following a zig-zagged course to protect the convoy from torpedoes. I was behind the gun when we passed the island of Negros and were near Mindanao when, very suddenly, the mast of a ship appeared on the horizon. Shortly thereafter another mast appeared. The ships were Japanese: one destroyer and either a light or a heavy cruiser some 33,000 yards away.

Faced with this first real threat of enemy action, my stomach contracted, my throat felt dry and adrenalin seemed to pour through my veins, making my heart beat like Kipling's sunrise.

"You scared?" asked O'Neil.

When I looked at him, I had to laugh and immediately felt calmer: he was as white as a cotton boll.

"Sure, I'm scared," I confessed. "So are you. You're whiter than a ghost!"

"You're pale, too. We shoulda stayed in bed, but no, we gotta be big heroes and join up. Coupla knotheads who had to save the day."

Admiral Glassford sent the *Paul Jones* to investigate. The loss of our essential cargo in a battle with the enemy could be very costly for us. He was not anxious for a showdown with the Japanese at this point. Apparently the Japs were not eager to fight, either. As soon as the three detached ships caught sight of ours, they increased their speed to lengthen the range and were soon out of sight. Since they could only be enemy ships, the *Paul Jones* pursued them to make sure they were not hovering nearby. They were apparently part of the enemy force which was making the initial landing on Mindanao.

This took place on the 11th. On the afternoon of the 12th, we were nearing the coast of North Borneo when the lookouts, who were somewhat tense from the scare of the day before, were told that someone on the *Langley* had sighted what appeared to be an enemy periscope. It was black and kept appearing and disappearing.

The *Langley*, carrying a cargo of gold and being in the most vulnerable position, did not hesitate to open fire at once. The ships of the convoy dispersed, with all guns alerted. A sigh of relief went up when it was determined that the enemy "periscope" was, in fact, not a periscope at all, but a piece of bamboo, waterlogged at one end, which rose and fell with the wave.

We passed the Sulu Islands on the 13th and entered the Makassar Strait, between Borneo and the Celebes. On the following day, we crossed the equator and, on the 15th, arrived on Balikpapan.

The ships anchored here and spent the night taking on fuel. We also spent the night with two somewhat unwelcome diversions. The mosquitoes were enormous and thick as fleas on a farm dog. When we were not trying to fight them off, we were struggling against the oppressive heat and humidity. We scarcely had time to think about the war.

We arrived in Soerbaja, Java on the 17th. We stayed on board the first night but, on the second night, I joined a liberty party and went ashore. The Dutch were very friendly, but did not try to disguise the fact that they feared our ships would attract Japanese planes. The natives seemed genuinely pleased to see us and did not appear to share the apprehension of the Dutch. The half-caste Javanese women were very beautiful, with light tan, blemish-free skin and huge, dark, attractive eyes. I thought of Estrelita, with whom I had enjoyed many pleasant interludes and wondered how she had fared in the bombing of Manila—or if I would ever see her again.

Native men and women alike stood about making V for victory signs, or displaying thumbs-ups. Their friendliness was heartwarming, particularly to a group of apprehensive sailors and marines who wondered what the next day held for them. It was the last friendliness any of us would know for a long, long time.

CHAPTER 3

Battle of the Flores Sea

On December 23, we resumed our voyage. The destination was Darwin, Australia. We had Christmas dinner here. Unlike the Dutch, the Aussies were delighted to see us and tried in every way to make us feel at home. Despite the fact that they were under strict wartime rationing, they extended invitations for us to visit in their homes, and included us in their plans for parties and other social activities.

We thought the Aussie women heavier than their American counterparts and the dress styles appeared to be about ten years behind those in the States. Their verbal expressions were odd, but quite intriguing. They used slang freely, often the same words that were common in American, but I discovered the hard way that their meaning was sometimes entirely different.

One evening, while on liberty, a marine buddy and I joined some Aussie acquaintances in a small "pub" in Darwin. One of the Aussies introduced me to a very attractive Australian girl in their party. After a short conversation, I asked her to dance.

"I would love to dance," she murmured ruefully, "but I am knocked up."

I could not believe my ears, which were flaming red by this time and asked her to repeat what she had said. I had heard right the first time. I must not have hidden my discomfort very well, because my marine buddy asked me if something was wrong. I told him I had to talk to him alone for a few minutes. We excused ourselves and went to the front of the pub. I told him the girl I had been paired off with was pregnant, and I was anxious to get away from her. He was equally stunned and called the Aussie who had introduced us.

"Say, bud, what's the idea of getting my friend a girl who is in the family way?"

The Aussie was completely puzzled, and asked what he was talking about. I explained. The Aussie roared with laughter. He asked me to repeat what the girl had told him. I complied

"Knocked up means she is tired and you must wait a few minutes for her to rest," he explained, between bouts of laughter.

I hastened to explain to him that that expression in Texas meant something far different. Everyone had a good laugh at my expense.

I enjoyed my liberties here, but the *Houston* soon finished her assignment in Darwin and began convoy duty to Thursday Island. On New Year's Day, we began our voyage and, upon arriving at Thursday Island, took over two troop ships which had been under the care of the *Pensacola*. These we convoyed to Darwin, and our convoy duty continued between these points and Java until February 2, 1942.

On February 2, the *Houston* joined the strike force that consisted of the *Marblehead*, the Dutch cruisers, *De Ruyter* and *Tromp*, two Dutch destroyers and six American destroyers.

There was no sign of the enemy in the sky or on the sea. We were beginning to grow restless. It seemed to me that this was a war of hide and seek with no one ever getting caught. A war without a battle. The only enemy ships we had seen had disappeared before we could get a good look at them and the only enemy planes had been allowed to continue on their mission because we had other fish to fry.

My duty as rammerman continued. On February 3, while I was on watch at the 5-inch battery. A wave of Jap aircraft was sighted off the *Houston*'s port bow. They were about 30,000 feet up, but the number of planes could not be determined because of the clouds. We were in a small bay near Timor and, not wishing to be discovered here, withheld fire. These planes were on their first mission to bomb Soerbaja. We were en route to Java to intercept a Jap convoy reported to be heading through the Makassar Strait.

We had many serious talks about home and the danger that threatened us constantly, but despite the fact that it was 0100, and we felt that a battle with the enemy was imminent, as we steamed out of the bay, we were wide awake and cheerful.

I met Chuck on deck on the morning of the 5th.

"It's been a month since Pearl Harbor, "he complained. "Damned if I ever heard of a war where you didn't have any fighting. I feel as useless as tits on a boar. Besides that, my feet hurt."

Chuck had scarcely uttered those words when, at 1030, waves of Jap bombers were sighted overhead. We counted 27 of them. Our ship immediately deployed full speed ahead, general quarters was sounded and the Japs came at us down to 18,000 feet. This time we let go as shells from the strike force peppered their formations, damaging a great number of their planes. The *Houston* was now in her first battle of the war. I was seeing and participating in my first fight of air and sea.

The *Houston* made a number of firing runs, and the battle raged for an hour before any of our ships was damaged. Then it happened … suddenly, the *Houston* was hit by a 500-pound bomb. It struck the main mast, went through the radio shack, the searchlight control room and exploded just above the main deck, aft of the number three turret.

When the bomb first struck it tore away the huge battle flag from the main mast. One of the sailors rushed to a demolished whaleboat, found a small flag, took a piece of cord from his pocket and secured the flag to the stanchion along the lifeline in the after part of the ship.

Our crew was alert and collected in the face of this first real danger. No one can minimize what a bomb that size can inflict. It wrought more havoc than we cared to admit, not only in the physical structure of the ship, but in casualties and in our first fatalities.

Bucket brigades were formed to flood the burning magazines. We had to control the flames before the wounded could be reached. One officer in the damaged turret had only his shoes left uncharred, while all of the other men in that location were burned beyond recognition. Commander Roberts, the ship's executive officer, removed his blouse and entered the burning magazine to assist the wounded out and to help remove the dead. Everyone worked where he was needed, disregarding rank and trying to assist the doctors and corpsmen in any way possible. We had 46 dead and 40 seriously wounded from burns and shrapnel, yet, despite this disaster, Captain Rooks kept the *Houston* on a battle course and the guns continued to fire.

As I look back, I guess we were lucky at that. When the bomb struck, I was in the 5-inch magazine, two decks below the spot where it exploded. When it was dropped it first struck the top of the mainmast, setting its timing apparatus in motion, causing it to explode before it hit the deck. Had this not happened and had it continued on its intended path, it would have hit the spot where I was on duty, igniting the larger supply of ammunition. The whole ship would have been blown to Kingdom Come.

The Japs seemed determined to knock out the *Houston* and the *Marblehead*, ignoring the Dutch ships and the other American ships. We had at this time four American, four British (*Jupiter, Encounter, Express, Electra*), four Dutch and four Australian destroyers (including the *Vampire*), and the Australian gunboats, *Jumna* and *Jarra*, all under command of Rear Admiral Doorman of the Royal Netherlands Navy.

The enemy increased the number of planes to 54, coming in in formations of nine. As they assaulted the Allied Fleet, the ships scattered, making it difficult for the Japs to make contact. But they were successful in unloading two bombs on the *Marblehead*. One large bomb hit her aft, shattering her steering gear and setting her afire. She suffered serious damage from the near miss. She was badly crippled, her rudder jammed and she was able to move only in circles. Two destroyers closed about her and began towing her toward Tjilatjap, Java. In grave danger of sinking, we did not expect to see her again. She had 13 men dead and 60 wounded.

The enemy planes had not fared well and were now anxious to get out of firing range. They departed as quickly as they had come. One plane had fallen not far from the *Houston* and a dying pilot could be seen caught on a detached wing of his plane, blood pouring from his wound and staining the sea around him, but there was no time to give him more than a glance.

Right after the second explosion on the *Marblehead*, I saw Strong, Jones and a sailor carrying a slender, olive drab-clad figure from the steaming magazine. Strong's face was set and very white and tears were streaming unchecked down Jones' face. I was still too busy with the gun at this point to have time to find out what was up.

Finally freed from my duties at the gun, I began to help with the wounded. I could see that some of the men who were being carried out were beyond help. Many of them were moaning and writhing in agony. I helped Chaplain Gray hold a burly sailor who had had both legs almost blown off, until either the shot he had been given or the loss of blood he sustained made him become quiet. Chuck Satterlee, with blood streaming down one side of his face, was helping an ensign carry a charred bundled that had, just a few minutes ago been a man, toward the fantail.

Some of my best friends were lying under canvas beneath that fantail. Pine boxes were being constructed for the bodies. Our ship was strangely quiet. I, who somehow had escaped, could find no reason to smile. Everyone went about his duty grimly. Even the chaplains, who were the most sought-after men on the ship, moved about quietly and in silent prayer.

When I wasn't on duty, I stood for long periods at the rail, staring into the water, my thoughts whirling. I was joined almost at once by Father Alvarez and Gunner McCann. The father held out a St. Christopher medal in the palm of his right hand.

"Tom O'Neil asked me to give this to you," he said, quietly, looking so much older than I remembered.

I stared at the tiny medal in astonishment. On the point of asking why, I stopped myself when it suddenly dawned on me: the only reason Tom would send anyone that medal would be because he had no further use for it. I couldn't stop a sob from escaping.

"When did it happen, father?" I managed to ask.

"Toward the start of the attack. He was in the magazine, but he didn't suffer long. Don't look so sad, my son. God had his reason for taking him now."

"He was one of the lucky ones," said McCann.

It had been the intention of the Allied Fleet to intercept the Japanese Navy at Balikpapan. This was out of the question for the time being without the assistance of the two major units. At the same time, we later learned, the U.S. Navy had carried out the first offensive action of the war against the Japanese. Another convoy under the command of Vice-Admiral William F. Halsey, Jr. raided Japanese bases on the Marshall and Gilbert islands.

Our own strike force was broken up by the Jap air assault. The *Houston* retired from the area and started towards Tjilatjap for repairs. We came upon the harbor very suddenly. Tjilatjap could scarcely be detected until we were upon her because of the topography of the surrounding terrain. Things here seemed quite normal. You would scarcely have known a war was in progress. Ships of many nations were in port. They bore Russian, Nicaraguan, Dutch, English and American flags. Russian woman were vigorously scrubbing the decks of merchant ships. A Dutch hospital ship pulled alongside us and received our seriously wounded. These were placed under the care of a Dr. Wassell.

There was little said by any of us this night. What would the morrow hold—or the next day—or the day after that? No one would venture a thought. But, of one thing I was certain: war had suddenly changed from an exciting adventure to a heart-sinking, horrible reality.

On February 7, we stood in the hot Javanese sunshine while funeral services were held for the men killed on the *Houston*. The ship's band played "Nearer My God to Thee" and "Eternal Father, Strong to Save." The flag-draped caskets were carried down the gangplank and interred in the muddy soil of Java.

In the afternoon, to everyone's astonishment, the *Marblehead* came limping into port. As she pulled alongside the *Houston*, the order was given to stand by and salute, but, instead of saluting, we waved, shouted and threw our caps into the air, giving them a rousing greeting. Cheers and roars came back from the *Marblehead*.

Since the living quarters of the *Marblehead*'s crew had been badly damaged, we took them aboard the *Houston*. They removed the battle grime, and after showering and being fed, we scrambled about finding new clothes for them from our own lockers. Theirs was shredded, to put it mildly.

Funeral services for the dead from the *Marblehead* were conducted on February 9. Following this, Admiral Hart and Sir Archibald Wavell came aboard to inspect the damage of the two heavy cruisers. It was obvious that the *Marblehead* had no alternative but to return to the United States, but the *Houston*, despite the fact that her stern turret looked like a tea strainer with 196 holes in it, would have to remain.

Admiral Hart departed for Washington and General Wavell assumed Supreme Command of the theater. A Dutch vice-admiral, Helfrich, took Admiral Hart's place as Commander of the Allied Naval Forces. As we started toward Darwin and before we saw Java again, our Allied headquarters were transferred to Tjilajap, on the southern coast of Java.

On February 15 the *Houston* had convoy duty. We were escorting four merchant ships loaded with supplies and equipment. At 0600, an enemy radio message was picked up: "Houston and four transports leaving for advanced base." At 0930, we sighted a lone, four-engine Jap bomber on the horizon at about 10,000 feet. We had three calls to general quarters before this plane finally made a firing run at 1100. We expended 200 rounds of ammunition before we finally brought it into the sea. By this time, it had accomplished its mission and radioed our position to the enemy.

We knew there would be another battle with the enemy planes. We had been standing watch, day and night, with little sleep since February 1 and could have done very well without another battle. We were aware that we were fighting a defensive war against numerically superior forces and, as conditions grew worse instead of better, we were all on the verge of collapse. I could not recall ever having been as weary. Every bone, muscle, joint and sinew seemed to ache with fatigue.

There was no sign of the enemy for the rest of the day, but it was bound to happen. It could not be otherwise—and it did. The next day, late in the afternoon, 44 enemy bombers came into sight. Ten of these were four-engined, the rest two-; they split into groups of seven or less and came at us. The order had been given to stand by. Our range-finder officer, Marine Captain Ramsey (who had taught us before hostilities broke out) always spoke slowly and softly. We had never seen him flustered, and today was no exception. If he hoped to keep us calm by example, he succeeded, in most cases, at least. Today, with planes coming in from every direction, we waited for his instructions. Finally, someone became anxious and asked over the phone, "Which group, captain?" We watched the captain survey the sky filled with enemy planes, in a slow, nonchalant manner, as though he had 44 mosquitoes under surveillance. Finally, he dropped his gaze to the *Houston's* deck and drawled, "Well … Hell! It doesn't matter." Then, he added, conversationally, "It looks like they are coming in from *every* direction."

In the ensuing battle, we shot down seven enemy planes. The *Houston's* fire power kept the planes too high to be effective. The only casualty was a seaman from one of the merchant ships who was killed by shrapnel from a near miss.

The skipper had sent a request for air support when he first sighted the planes. Two hours later, one lone P-40 fighter appeared and radioed, "Are you alright?"

The captain, annoyed by the lack of air support, returned with more than a touch of sarcasm, "Yes. Are you?"

We could not continue on our mission. We had expended half of our ammo in two days of fighting. We were now in the Flores Sea, two days away from Timor. The skipper had been informed that the Japanese had already effected landings on the islands southwest of Timor. There, land-based planes could demolish us and the convoy, so we retraced our course to Darwin.

We made a hurried trip and with new supplies, left Darwin on February 19 and none too soon. We received a message that Darwin was bombed six hours after our departure. We had no illusions about the danger ahead, as we sailed toward Tjilajap. Many Allied ships, transports, and destroyers had been sunk, as had a Dutch hospital ship. The few who had not drowned, or been devoured by sharks, had been mercilessly strafed in the water by the Jap flyers.

We refueled at Tjilajap and, on February 22, we started back into the danger area. Proceeding through the Sunda Straits, into the Java Sea, we arrived at Soerbaja just in time to participate in a number of enemy air attacks. The Japs were eager to take the island and we were interfering with their landing plans. We were a thorn in their side and had given two good demonstrations of what heavy cruiser fire power could accomplish. We expected strong enemy countermeasures.

During the air attacks at Soerbaja, the Dutch sailors went ashore and took cover in the air raid shelters. Our ship was the only one firing, period. While trying valiantly to keep the planes at a high altitude, the skipper received a message from the Dutch government demanding that we cease firing: the shells were damaging houses and other buildings The *Houston* continued to fire.

The air raids continued throughout the next four days, and then we joined the strike force that consisted of the *De Ruyter*, the *Exeter*, the *Java*, the *Perth*, and ten destroyers, five of which were American, three British, and two Dutch. Now we were eager for a showdown with the Jap fleet.

CHAPTER 4

Battle of the Java Sea

We hadn't long to wait. We stayed at our stations day and night. Dangerously near breaking point from lack of sleep, we had had no full meals, just a belly full of battle fatigue. By the fourth day, I was numb from exhaustion, my head ached and my eyes felt as though they had had sand sprinkled into them. The only thing that kept me going was the knowledge that everyone else felt the same way. The enemy raids had damaged docks and ships and one ship with a rubber cargo lay burning in the harbor.

Then it happened. All weariness and pain vanished instantly.

Late in the afternoon, Allied scout planes reported the position of the Jap fleet. The strike force changed its course and steamed out into battle formation. In a short while, the Battle of the Java Sea began.

We could see the enemy fleet about 30,000 yards away. It was composed of five heavy cruisers and between 20 and 30 destroyers.

The order came: "Commence firing."

The *De Ruyter* opened fire and the *Houston* followed immediately. Our line of fire straddled the Jap ships for two salvos. The third salvo set one of the Jap heavy cruisers on fire. She appeared to be stricken and the last time I saw her she was trying to get out of range of our fire. Another Jap cruiser was set ablaze by the combined fire power of the *De Ruyter* and the *Exeter*. The *Perth* and the *Java* were not effective at that range, but were successful to a degree in keeping the Japanese destroyers at a sufficient distance to prevent their firing torpedoes into the Allied ships.

The *Exeter*, however, was the first Allied ship to take a torpedo amidships and was forced to abandon the fight. The *Houston* was hit twice, first on the forecastle, penetrating two decks of the officers' quarters and the forward hull of the ship, damaging the forward small stores and living compartments. The second struck portside, hitting an oil tank amidships.

At 1830 both sides retired to make ready for a night battle. Both fleets had lost destroyers and submarines, but it was our belief that we had won the battle; consequently, our morale was very high. We felt, generally, that we had acquitted ourselves honorably.

At 2100 the battle resumed. I was behind my gun. Admiral Doorman, who was now in command, ordered an attack on a Jap cruiser and transport force. It was an odd sensation for me as I watched the beautiful flashes from the huge enemy guns on the horizon. This changed to an eerie and very apprehensive feeling as Jap shells began to whiz overhead and splash in the water nearby. Some of the shells came so close that drops of water struck me in the face.

We were giving the Japs their fair share, however. Our 5-inch battery was firing star shells over the target and the 8-inch guns were inflicting much damage. The Japs began to retire, whereupon Admiral Doorman ordered the Allied ships to follow. His flagship, the *De Ruyter*, in hot pursuit, steamed ahead and there was nothing for us to do but to follow. We had sent a destroyer back to Soerbaja for more torpedoes and when our skipper received the order to follow the Jap ships unescorted, he could not believe the Admiral was in earnest. It was obvious that the enemy had large forces in the area and our skipper felt there must be some mistake in the message.

The four ships proceeded as ordered, despite our feeling that this was suicidal. In a short while, it became abundantly evident that we had been lured into a submarine nest. The Japs sent out long strings of blinker flares, their scouting planes attempting to use both these and regular flares to show us clearly to their submarine fleet. In very short order, the *De Ruyter* was struck by a torpedo and torn apart. A tremendous blast resulted and the entire area lit up. Within minutes the *Java* suffered a like fate and this, too, resulted in a terrific blast which outlined our ships to the enemy like sitting ducks.

Our two remaining ships, the *Houston* and the *Perth*, lost no time in retiring from the area. It was obvious that, with torpedoes coming from every direction, it would only be a matter of minutes until we, too, would be blown from the water. It was decided that we would try to reach Tjilatjap via the Indian Ocean. As both ships headed out of the combat zone, I was still at my battle station on the boat deck. The *Houston*, with submarines on either side, had stopped to listen for aircraft. The *Perth* had been coming alongside at a very fast rate of speed, and as the *Houston* started ahead once more, she cut directly across our path. Our officer on the *Houston*'s bridge saw her just in time and the order rang out, "Full speed astern!" We barely avoided a collision! To all of us, this was by far the greatest alarm of the day.

On the following day, we reached Batavia without incident, at 1500, stopping there to take on fuel. A scout sea plane appeared on the horizon, but since it appeared to be an American plane, we were not alerted. In a short while, one of our planes was released to do some patrolling. At about 1700, when our plane was due to return, what appeared to be an American plane flew overhead. Suddenly, while we were still looking at it, and before we could get into firing position, the plane slipped in and dropped two 100-pound bombs on the deck. Shortly thereafter our plane returned, and, taking no chances, this time, we opened fire. It was far enough away to avoid the shell fire, but the perplexed pilot sent the following radio message: "What the hell is going on?" We gave him the signal to come in, and he complied with much relief.

We had been in Batavia barbor for three and a half hours and were still unable to take on any fuel. Our skipper was afraid the enemy would cut off our escape through the Sunda Straits and a Dutch plane was sent out to investigate. The pilot reported back that there were no enemy ships in or near the Straits. This was good news and we anticipated no trouble.

The news that there were no enemy ships in the area was just what we needed. For the first time in more days than I cared to calculate, we had time to take a shower. I even dragged my mattress topside, hoping to get a little sleep. A month of constant alerts, very little food and very little sleep had taken a toll on all of us. Although we were battle-weary and red-eyed, we were quite cheerful. We even speculated about liberty in Perth, Australia, which is where we hoped we were headed. I fell asleep just aft of my gun.

CHAPTER 5

"No Enemy Ships in the Straits"

Our relief was short-lived. Our two ships set Condition X-Ray and headed away from the area. I had been asleep for almost an hour when we started through the Sunda Straits. Word went round that something had been sighted just ahead. I picked up my shoes and ran to my gun. The *Perth* blinked her battle lights, just as a precautionary measure. In return there came the incorrect signal, and both the *Perth* and the *Houston* realized simultaneously that we had followed a Jap convoy into the Straits. The *Perth* opened fire at once.

My first thought was of the Dutch bomber that had given such an optimistic report about no enemy ships in the Straits. Looking about me, I saw dozens of dark silhouettes, which I hoped could not be enemy ships but, as the guns opened up, I saw destroyers, cruisers and many enemy transports. They were making an unopposed landing on the Java coast. We concentrated our fire on the transports first, but the range was extremely short and our 5-inch guns began firing point blank at torpedo boats. The *Houston* continued to fire her 8-inch guns, local control, at the enemy ships. We succeeded in sinking two Jap ships before we sustained any serious damage.

In the confusion and because of the short range, the enemy ships began firing at each other. After 20 minutes of battle, the *Perth* sank, leaving the *Houston* to fight alone. The Jap ships, seeing their advantage, came in at close range to our stern, which was unprotected because of our disabled number three turret. Many of the sailors and marines on board our ship began using machine guns and pistols. One of the Jap transports had turned over in the water and the screams of the drowning men rent the air. The enemy concentrated their fire on our bridge and the 8-inch forward battery.

The *Houston* began to list badly. Something was wrong in the 5-inch magazine and we did not have sufficient ammunition to keep the battery going. Finally, having had a great deal of experience in the magazine, I left my gun to go below to see if I could speed up delivery of the ammunition. I found one of the men had passed out. Seven others were working under tremendous strain. It was hellishly hot. The men were stripped to their waist, and I, too, stripped and piled in to help. The shells weighed about 70 pounds each and were very bulky to handle. In a short time, my shoes were soaked, my clothes wringing wet, and there were puddles of perspiration on the steel deck around us. The skin was torn from our fingers and wrists but we managed to keep two hoists going. The ship was listing badly and there was a continual thud of shells. I began to wonder how many shells a ship could take and still remain afloat.

The ship began going round and round in circles. We received hoarse orders from the men above, "Send up star shells!" then, '"Hold port," "Start starboard!" We worked furiously giving no thought to the outcome. We had no time for thought. The shells were almost gone and water was seeping into the magazine. The *Houston* had taken a torpedo on the starboard side amidships and, seconds later, she took another on the port side, amidships again. The engine rooms were flooded and wrecked. All over the ship could be heard the screams of men who were being suffocated and burned to death.

Then came the order from Captain Rooks, terse and final: "Abandon ship!"

The shells were almost gone by the time the order came and water continued to seep into the magazine. When we reached topside, the skipper told us to return to our station. He said that he would try to beach the *Houston* and use her as a shore battery.

We complied with his request, but before Captain Rooks could carry out his plan, the ship took another torpedo on the starboard side amidships; almost immediately afterward, she took another on the port side amidships. Speed was instantly reduced. Captain Rooks, with only 100 rounds of 5-inch ammunition and much less 8-inch gave the second order to abandon ship.

While working in the magazine during the last phase of the battle, we were kept informed about the general situation topside. The reports came down by phone: "Three torpedo boats blown to hell!" The damage inflicted on the enemy was reported as well as the shells taken by the *Houston*. When the *Houston* took a shell, there was a low, rumbling sound. When we went topside after the first order to abandon ship I was stunned by the altered appearance of the ship. From the looks of things on deck, it appeared that every part of her had taken a shell.

When the second order to abandon ship came, the bugler sounded the call without a falter in any note. He did not survive. On the way down from the bridge the skipper was struck in the back by a piece of shrapnel and instantly killed ... but every man on board had heard his last order, "Abandon ship!"

All over the upper decks and bridges and in the compartments below decks, men died. The ladders had been blown away from the forward machine-gun nest and the men left had a very difficult time getting down. Finally, with shells and even bullets coming from every direction, they managed to slide down the leg of the tripod mast.

Although the order had been given to abandon ship, we were caught in a flooded magazine two decks below the water line. Two of the shell compartments were flooded and both hatches had been bolted down to keep the water out of the hoist room. We managed to open the armored plate hatch ten feet above us, but the hatch on the next deck was closed securely and bolted down. There was no way that we could open it from our location. Water poured into the magazine. We could only conclude that this was the end of the magazine crew. At least, I told myself, we would be drowned, not killed by the enemy, but this was cold comfort. I suddenly found that I had no desire to die by any means. I was not yet twenty.

Everyone on board was, no doubt, busily trying to save his own neck. I had had one narrow escape. I had no reason to assume that I could be that fortunate again. Every man, me included, was praying. Men pray hard and earnestly under these conditions. Some of the men had never prayed before, but they did now. And it looked, momentarily, as though our prayers would be answered.

Suddenly, there was the sound of a hatch being unbolted and, looking up, I saw what I thought must be an angel, but was in reality the face of Marine Corporal Faulk, who had risked his own life to run back and unbolt the hatch, thus saving the entire magazine crew. He had been my friend for some time, but from that day he was the man who had saved my life.

We lost no time getting topside. Two other marines, Owens and Corsburg, and I, covered in oil, soot and sweat, clambered into a foot of water on the deck of the ship. Gaping torpedo holes and shell holes made her sides look like a cheese grater. Enemy search lights blazed across her decks. Jap ships steamed back and forth, firing at will at the stricken *Houston*. It struck me that they were gloating over the death of the flagship. Three times in the last month our radio had picked up enemy reports that the *Houston* had just been sunk. This time, they were taking no chances.

I looked overboard and seeing the great expanse of saltwater, suggested that we find a drinking fountain, if possible. We found one still in working order and drank gratefully. As we returned topside, I found a wounded sailor lying in a lifeboat and cut him loose, hoping he would float free as the ship went down. He was badly wounded and it would obviously be quite impossible for him to swim, just as it would be impossible for us to take him with us overboard.

There were no life preservers or life rafts available and the dark, oily waters beneath the sinking ship seemed the only desperate means of escape. The Japs continued to fire at the ship and we needed no one to tell us that it was not a safe place to be. We had another problem, however, when we learned that Corsburg could not swim. He refused to leave the ship with us and we refused to leave without him. We were standing on the fantail just over the propeller screws, trying to persuade him when a salvo landed just behind us, and we jumped.

Once in the cold water, we removed everything but our shorts to facilitate swimming. Our teeth began to chatter and we suffered from cramps. I began to realize how completely exhausted I was. We knew the Java coast was some distance away, but had no idea how far, or in which direction. Jap destroyers circled about firing at everything that moved. We were close enough to them to see the spray from their suction. Projectiles whistled over our heads and passed near us in the water. The concussion from the guns was deafening and almost unbearable.

The last we saw of Corsburg, he was still standing on the deck of the *Houston* staring into the water. He had not jumped with us. The ship was sinking slowly. She was still brightly lit by enemy searchlights. On top of the mainmast the American flag fluttered bravely in the tropical night. It was, indeed, our only symbol of hope.

As the *Houston* went to her grave, the last thing I saw was the American flag … and the marine standing on her shattered deck.

★

On Sunday morning, March 1, 1942, a new life began for many of us. The only home we had in this part of the world was lying at the bottom of the Sunda Straits. Both Owens and I were good swimmers, but after swimming for what seemed like an hour we were getting panicky. Along with our splashing and the sound of guns, we could hear the cries of the wounded and dying coming from all sides. A thick layer of oil covered the water, coating our bodies, filling our eyes and inhibiting our ability to float. We could make out the dim outline of the Java coastline, but it appeared to be a considerable distance away. At intervals, we passed swimmers in the area who uttered strange cries in a tongue I recognized as Japanese. These we knew must be soldiers from the two Japanese troop ships which the *Houston* had managed to sink before going to her own doom.

Suddenly, my hand struck an object floating in the water and, instinctively, I clung to it. It proved to be a life raft and we climbed aboard, thrilled with our good fortune. Once safely aboard, we floated about among the Jap ships, looking for survivors from the *Houston*, particularly the severely wounded. We soon had three badly burned men aboard. The raft would not hold more than three men lying prostrate. Besides ourselves we contacted 24 others who clung to the sides of the raft. Some of these had serious wounds and were chilled from long exposure in the icy water, but huddling together seemed to warm them and protect them somewhat from the bone-chilling breeze.

I was worried about sharks but the misery of listening to the wounded and dying and their shrill, agonizing shrieks, when I had nothing to give them for their pain, soon took my mind off of my own problems. The Japs had resumed their landing operations and callously ignored the hundreds of suffering men in the water, although many were their own.

The most seriously burned man on our raft cried piteously for water, but we had none to give him. A chaplain, G. S. Rentz, from the *Houston*, tried to calm him, talking to him in low, soothing tones. Finally, he lapsed into a delirium. He was critically burned. The chaplain removed his own life jacket and placed it beside one of the burned men. He kept telling us that he was an older man and would give his space on the raft to someone who had a longer span before him. He said he was not afraid to die. We thought we had dissuaded him, but toward morning, someone spoke to him and found that he was not there. No one had noticed, but during the night, he had apparently released his grip on the raft and quietly disappeared.

Miserably cold, wet, hungry and covered from head to foot in a thick coating of oil, we continued to float about among the Jap ships. After what seemed like an eternity, dawn began to tinge the eastern sky with a rosy hue, revealing that our raft was hopelessly overcrowded. The most seriously burned man died and I removed the life jacket from his body. I was determined to try to swim to the Java coast to lessen the load on the raft. The sun rose and another man became delirious.

I swam for almost three miles and felt that I would achieve my goal when, suddenly, near the shore, I was caught in a wicked current that threatened to carry me out to sea. I had no choice but to head back to the raft. On my return, I passed a number of Jap corpses floating in the water and, occasionally, an American or Australian body. There was still no attempt to rescue survivors. In the daylight, I was astounded to see how many Jap ships were participating in the landing operation. At least the *Houston* had been opposed by a tremendously overwhelming enemy force.

I was sure that when the Dutch realized the Japs were trying to land on the Java, no doubt they would quickly push the enemy back into the sea. But where were they? Swimming alone back to the raft, I had time to think about the *Houston*. She had been President Roosevelt's favorite warship. He had used her for several fishing trips and had sent her on a goodwill cruise to Japan. The Japanese had sent their planes out to take pictures of her while she was in Tokyo Bay. Now she lay at the bottom of the Straits. Depression settled over me.

When I reached the raft my fingers were so numb that holding on to the edge was a challenge. The oil and saltwater had gotten into my eyes and made them burn, painfully. I looked at the men hanging on to the life raft and decided they were as sorry-looking a group as I had ever seen. A decapitated corpse floated by and, in a moment, another. They were Australians. I wondered whether the Japs or the natives had killed them and had no illusions that there might be great danger ahead for all of us.

CHAPTER 6

Samurai Hospitality

We circled the Jap ships. About midmorning a Japanese landing barge bearing three Jap soldiers began circling our raft, ogling us. At length, they turned back toward a Japanese ship and, after signaling and reviewing their orders, returned to pick up the survivors. Coming alongside us, they began jabbering in Japanese, but apparently realizing that we did not speak their language, they began to help one of the wounded men into the barge. Having done this, they sat back and watched the others—many of whom had broken arms or legs, or severe wounds—struggle in as best they could. This accomplished, they systematically stripped us of all rings, watches, money and knives we had managed to save. I watched the greedy expressions on their faces and experienced a feeling of revulsion. The enemy, however, seemed more than pleased with their loot and offered the men cigarettes. They turned the boat toward the Java coast.

It took the barge 30 minutes to reach the beach. I realized more than ever how fortunate I had been to find the raft. The barge stopped, and we alighted on a white, sandy beach. Under a grove of coconut palms, about 40 other prisoners were huddled together. Many of them were seriously wounded but no effort was made to treat them. I did not need to be told that some of them would soon be beyond treatment.

I found a place to sit down and soon rain began to pelt us. Since most of us were already soaked from our dip in the Straits, this did little to raise our sagging spirits. When it stopped, the air was chill and we began to turn blue. Jap guards stood about with their guns trained on us, but steadfastly refused to comply with our requests for food, water, or attention for our wounded. I arose and walked back and forth within the circle of guards to increase my circulation. Just as I began to grow warmer, the rain set in again. It continued for an hour this time, during which time several more prisoners arrived on an enemy barge.

There were now 78 men on the beach. Hungry, chilled to the bone, thirsty, covered with oil, groggy from lack of sleep and the events of the past several days, we sat forlornly watching the Jap landing operations.

After another three hours, a Japanese officer appeared, surveyed us coldly and said in English: "Hello! How are you?" Since the question was purely rhetorical, he did not wait for an answer, but started bombarding us with questions.

"What ship are you from?"

"The Houston" answered one of our officers.

The interrogator immediately slapped him in the face. "Why do you lie to me?" he asked, angrily. "The Houston has been sunk for many days."

"We have heard that, too, but the fact remains that it was sunk last night. Why should we lie to you?" our officer replied.

"You are Americans?"

"Yes."

"What ship are you from?"

"The Houston."

No slap this time. "How many men did you have?"

"Approximately a thousand," responded the officer.

"What was your mission?"

"Trying to prevent the Japanese from reaching the shores of Java."

"What was your destination?"

"Our destination was not known to us."

The Jap officer then proceeded to ask innumerable questions about the number of guns, the type of ship, its weight, and many details which to us seemed irrelevant in view of the fact that the *Houston* was sitting on the bottom of the Sunda Straits. At the end of each third or fourth question, he always repeated, like a parrot: "What ship were you on?"

Finally, someone, tired of the repetition, asked where he learned to speak English.

The Jap officer was obviously immensely pleased by this question. He immediately ordered cigarettes passed to the prisoners and became very chatty.

"I was graduated from the University of Washington in Seattle," he proudly asserted. "Most of my life, however, has been spent in San Francisco. I still have a wife and son there and hope I will soon return to them in the States. I am still making payments on an electric washing machine and a refrigerator there.

"The war will not last long," he confided. "The United States has been bombed, also Australia and the Philippines. Your fleet has been sunk. It will not be long until you can return to your homes."

With these final words of comfort, he left us. We all felt it would be a short war, but never in the days ahead did we doubt that the Allies would be victorious.

We continued to watch the Japs unload their ships. This was more encouraging to us than the Japs realized. It gave us an excellent opportunity to assess the enemy's equipment. It was our conclusion that the enemy had salvaged it from some World War I battlefield. Their mortars were 3-pound knee mortars, their artillery pieces horse-drawn and the rifles the cheapest obtainable. Even the equipment and supply-carrying trucks were dilapidated, and the consensus was that it would take the Dutch two days at the most to push the whole lot of them back into the sea.

By afternoon, the sun was very hot and we had more urgent concerns created by our great thirst and gnawing hunger. The tropical sun is quite capable of giving a man bad sunburn beneath two layers of clothing. Our naked shoulders were soon blistered and the breeze that had chilled us in the morning died away entirely, leaving us with a still, oppressive, humid heat that was almost suffocating. Perspiration trickled from our already dehydrated bodies and we became limp from lack of salt.

About mid-afternoon, the Jap officer from Seattle returned and ordered us to march down the road bordering the beach. The 12 guards assigned to us seemed to be in a particularly sadistic mood. A number of times I saw them use their rifle butts to viciously strike wounded men who were slower than the rest of us. A protesting American officer was slapped in the face by a guard and, when he persisted in his protestations, was brutally struck in the groin with the guard's rifle butt. None of the guards spoke English.

Bananas and coconuts grew all along the roadside but when the famished prisoners tried to pick some the guards struck them in the face with their fists or the flat side of their bayonets. A Japanese soldier stepped up to one of our shirtless men and, with a laugh, pulled on his chest hair. Looking at the small, bandy-legged guards, I began to calculate how many I could beat up in my exhausted condition. One of the guards, noticing my hairy chest, walked up even with me and, pulling at the hair, began to laugh wildly and jabber to his companions in Japanese. At first, I thought he had either read my thoughts or gone mad, but, looking at the smooth, brown arms and faces of the guards, I decided they were surprised at the amount of hair we had on our bodies. I tried to visualize an American behaving this way and concluded there must be a great difference between the mind of an Oriental and that of a Westerner. Where, I wondered, was the famous Japanese dignity?

The hot sun beat down upon the asphalt road, reflecting the glare back into our faces. We were all weak, hungry and blistered. Many were suffering from painful wounds. I was near collapse when we finally arrived at a small, red-tiled schoolhouse and the guards actually called a halt.

An area around the school was marked off and the guards, armed with machine guns, stationed themselves along the boundary. An American baking powder carton, 36″ x 24″ and about 18″ deep was placed before us on the ground. A guard threw ten green coconuts at our feet. We were ordered to eat. The box contained sour, cold rice. We dug the rice out into our hands and after eating it with our oil-coated fingers, broke the coconuts and passed them from man to man in order that each might wet his lips with the coconut milk. The meat of a green coconut is not something we found edible.

Our thirst could not be quenched with the minute amount of coconut milk and we went in search of water. A well on the premises proved to have a supply, but someone had used it as a latrine. Several of the men were feverish and parched with thirst. They drank the water in spite of its contaminated state.

Seventy-eight men could not fit inside the schoolhouse; therefore, it was obvious that it would not accommodate us as sleeping quarters. Someone asked one of the guards for permission to cut a coconut palm in order that those of us sleeping outside might use the leaves as a shelter against the heavy dew and damp cold of the rapidly approaching tropical night. Permission was granted.

A small hut had been previously constructed as a headquarters for the Japanese officers. They were busily occupied inside with their maps and plans, ostensibly plotting the demise of the Allied forces, when the prisoners who had been given the detail to cut down the palm tree began their chopping. The guard watching the cutting detail apparently knew little about chopping. He supervised them while they took time selecting the largest, tallest palm in the vicinity and carefully aimed its fall in the direction of the hut. Suddenly, and irretrievably, it fell with a great, rending crash directly atop the small, but strategic headquarters.

Japanese officers ran screaming from the hut like ants abandoning a disturbed nest, obviously under the impression that a bomb had fallen on the shack. We watched them scramble from the hut, shaking with fear, but this was quickly followed by rage as they saw what had happened and caught the POWs laughing until tears ran down their faces.

"For this you will work!" shouted one of the officers. He was furiously trying to regain "face" before the troops and the prisoners.

We were more pleased at this decision than he knew. It just might give us a chance to throw a few monkey wrenches into their plans. We much preferred working to sitting idle. We felt their control over our destinies was to be of short duration, but meanwhile we had enjoyed a joke at their expense and that bit of levity was sorely needed at that point.

I slept outside with a host of others. Despite my enormous fatigue, I lay wide awake for a long time under the stars. I was sure my parents would be notified that I was missing in action. How, I wondered, could I possibly get word to them? We conversed in whispers. Finally, we agreed that the Dutch offensive could not be long in getting underway.

There would, of course, be reprisals for the bold action of the Japs and we would be freed. They might even come tonight. We all needed sleep and it behooved us to be in the best possible shape to help them when they arrived. I fell asleep.

We were awakened before dawn by the guards dashing about screaming "*Kiwotsuke!*" which we later learned meant they wanted our attention. Since none of us spoke Japanese and all of us were stiff and sore for a number of reasons—not the least being our having slept on the cold ground all night—things did not move along as rapidly as our captors might have wished.

The guards, anxious to get us on our feet, began striking us with fists and rifle butts to hasten the action. It was a comedy of errors, not unlike a cruel farmer herding a flock of unruly sheep and goats. I was unable to repress a grin at the spectacle presented by the U.S. sailors, marines and their officers, wearing nothing but their undershorts and several days' growth, finally standing rigidly at attention before the tiny, irate Jap guards,. Most of them towered over their captors. Their expressions represented a wide variety of emotions, ranging from contempt to indignation, astonishment and bafflement.

After a few bad moments, it became apparent to us that the enemy's intention was to teach us to count off in Japanese. The guard repeated the word and the prisoner repeated it after him. We invariably failed to attain perfection on the first run and received a blow from the rifle butt of the guard. There were few of us, indeed, who bore no new cuts when the counting was ended. Each of the 12 guards counted us separately and since they frequently disagreed on our number, the total process took more than an hour. When each guard had finished his tally, a squabble broke out and a few extra tallies were needed to bring peace to the ranks. Abbott and Costello could not have done better.

When the tremendously complicated process of counting was finally completed we were marched along the road which we had traversed the previous day. Here, enemy barges were waiting and we were crowded into them en route to a merchant vessel in the bay. Once on board, we were lined up in four ranks on the quarterdeck. While we waited for instructions about our duties, the small guards pestered us, prodding us with their rifles and shrieking "*Kiwotsuke!*" It was a new experience for me to have a small, brown man, half the size of my kid brother rudely pushing me about and roaring insults in a strange tongue. At the age of 19, I had yet to develop endless patience when goaded.

"How would you like me to throw you overboard?" I asked him, smiling cheerfully. The tiny Jap, comprehending nothing in English, looked startled for a moment and I could have sworn he was on the verge of offering me a cigarette—although I did not smoke. Suddenly a Japanese captain appeared and we all straightened like scorched lizards, determined to make the best appearance possible, despite the sad condition of our "uniforms."

The captain wore horn-rimmed glasses, a beard, an olive drab uniform and what appeared to be a baseball cap beneath which all of his hair had been shaved like a kid whose mother had found nits in his hair. He was small in stature. His uniform had been tailored for a much larger man; its blouse made no pretense of following the contours of his upper torso; the seat of his trousers hung almost to the backs of his knees. He looked to be the prototype of what the well-dressed officer does not wear, but as some of the prisoners later commented, all of the padding and elevator shoes in Hollywood could not have changed the fact that he was shaped like a soft drink bottle. At the risk of seeming uncharitable, I must admit that I concurred. Despite his diminutive size, he was nothing if not forceful and he strode directly before us.

With a few Napoleonic mannerisms, he delivered this speech: "You are now prisoners of war!" He searched our faces to make sure, apparently, that this sank in sufficiently. Satisfied, he resumed his dialogue. "Japanese work—they work hard. You must work. You understand? Work! Work! Do you understand? We do not have bread and butter. We have rice, fish and barley. You will have that, but you must work. Work! Do you understand?

All of us nodded our heads politely and repeated in unison, "Yes, we understand."

The captain looked puzzled at our compliance, as though he had expected some protest. He scrutinized us searchingly for a few seconds and, apparently satisfied, waved his hand for us to be taken away.

It was nearing the noon hour and we were herded below decks where a meal of hot rice and potato stew flavored with soy sauce was waiting. Chopsticks and hot tea were provided. The temperature in the hold was about 111°. The food was clean, but unpalatable. I could not keep my mind from dwelling on a pitcher of ice water, but must admit that the tea tasted better than the half teaspoon of green coconut milk, which was all I had had in almost two days.

The guards and merchant seamen leered at us throughout the afternoon, throwing pieces of hard candy and cigarettes to us. We had the impression that they regarded us as some rare species of monkey just arrived from the Congo. One of the guards could speak some English and asked me where I had lived in the States. When I told him Texas, he nodded approvingly and repeated, again and again, not unlike a cracked record, "Texas, California and Washington," with an air of finality as though he had named all the states in the Union.

There was a vast difference between the guards and the merchant seamen. The latter had visited American ports, spoke relatively fluent English and, without question, realized the enormity of the task their country had set for herself in attacking us. Some of them talked eagerly to us.

"Japan is a small country," one told me. "She cannot win the war. Why do they talk so foolishly? America is very large!" He shook his head sadly.

Apparently the enemy was not yet prepared to give us a work detail. Despite the captain's insistence that we must emulate the Japanese and work, darkness settled on the hold and we were each tossed a straw mat upon which to sleep. This was our only bedding. We sat on the mats in the dark and whispered about our hopes for rescue until we finally fell asleep. Near midnight, we were brought to our feet, when, without warning, the ship's 5-inch guns opened fire.

"AIR RAID!" came from the lips of several of the panic-stricken men. What irony, I thought, to be killed in this enemy hold by bombs from our own planes.

"Don't make any noise or the guards will shoot. No disturbance whatever!" one of the officers told us.

We sat tensely in the darkness waiting for the bomb that would blow us to atoms. I reflected that the Allied planes would have no way of knowing that the ship carried prisoners and they would bomb indis-criminately. The planes must be very near, or the guns would not have opened up. We scarcely dared breathe, sitting motionless, listening for the sound of the planes.

The ship's guns ceased firing and all was quiet once again. After what seemed like hours, a guard opened a door to our quarters and was obviously shocked at the sight of all of us sitting rigidly upright on our mats. He shone his light from one man to the other and then asked what our problem was. When we told him we were expecting an air raid because the guns had been fired, he laughed uproariously. They were only having a drill, he explained, and no one had bothered to notify the prisoners.

We had pumped enough adrenalin in our systems to keep us awake for most of the night. I could not prevent the images of my two narrow escapes from floating through my mind; one, when by accident, a bomb struck the main mast of the *Houston* during the Battle of the Flores Sea and, again, when I had been trapped in the flooded magazine before the ship went down. It is difficult to have an optimistic outlook when a fellow is hungry, tired and harassed by the threat of imminent death; the fact that I did not know from which direction it might come, nor the means by which it might be achieved, did nothing to ease my fears.

We had our opportunity to work as soon as dawn broke on the following morning. We much preferred to work to maintain our stamina and we hoped it would give us some opportunity to do a bit for the Allied effort by sabotage. Although we could scarcely be classed as in prime condition for hard labor, we were pleased to be given a breakfast of hot rice and stew and transported to the docks where we were told to unload the Jap ships.

We were anxious to work on the ships, knowing there might be an opportunity to sabotage the enemy's stores and machinery. The work, however, was hard and the weather very hot. My hands were also very sore. My previously injured fingers and wrists were now infected. I could have used some bandages and a pair of work gloves, but managed to help unload cases of ammunition of all kinds, bombs, gasoline, medical equipment, beer and saki. On occasion one of our prisoners managed to steal a bottle of beer and drink it behind a stack of boxes in a corner.

At noon, we had another meal composed of rice and the same stew and returned to the docks. I had almost constant sharp hunger pangs. The food was issued in servings too small to appease my hunger. No doubt it was sufficient for the small Japs, but I needed no one to tell me I could not keep my 6′ 2″ frame at its 185-pound average without supplemental nourishment. Most of the prisoners were from Texas or adjoining states. Few were small men. We had complained about food on the *Houston* as a matter of course. It certainly did not taste like that of our mothers, but compared to this, it had been a three-times-daily banquet.

During the afternoon, we unloaded some rations. We hoped to steal something, but the choices were rather limited, consisting of horse meat, hard tack and small, sour, red canned plums. I passed up the first two and after sampling the third, decided the pains were not as severe as they had been.

At evening chow we were given a sardine between three men in addition to the rice and stew. The stew was given a variety of names by the men, most of them unrepeatable. Most of us used chopsticks, no doubt in ways in which they had never been used previously, since they frequently crossed and we dropped one or both or used our hands. One sailor persisted in declaring at each meal that he wished all the chopsticks in sight were inside the Jap officers and, at the end of the war, intended to see that some of them were. Another, taking issue with his language, suggested he try purifying his mind and his soul. He replied that he had been on a fast for too long already, religious or otherwise, and his girl would not be able to recognize him in his blues if he looked like Mohandas Gandhi.

We were given a treat after chow; namely, a saltwater shower. Some of the men swore the enemy had allowed us this privilege in self-defense, but whatever the reason, it was welcome. The water felt wonderful as we tried to remove the grime and oil from our blistered skins, and then … the salt got into the blisters. A howl went up like a choir of cats on the backyard fence at midnight.

Despite the fact that the showers had not removed the oil since we had no soap, we felt well enough the next day to contrive some sabotage against the enemy. We cheerfully unloaded the ships, at the same time pouring sugar in the gasoline, or stacking the barrels upside down with loosened caps, dropping boxes of ammo overboard and throwing away tiny, vital pieces of machinery. Had we been caught, we would have sustained a severe beating, but we made sure that there was an adequate number of lookouts and none of us was caught. In nine days we were able to unload 40 ships.

When we finished the ships we had time to think about our situation with more concern. Where were the Dutch? How could such a landing force manage to complete an operation with no resistance whatsoever from the local army or populace? We had seen no new prisoners arrive and no evidence of resistance from the Allies. We went to our mats on the last night wondering "What's next?" "Where are the prisoners from the Perth?" "Why doesn't someone free us?" "Surely this has gone on long enough. It is time for some reprisals!" "Where are the Dutch?"

CHAPTER 7

Serang, Java: Not Even a Chancre Mechanic

Finally, on March 12, I saw some evidence of Dutch resistance. We were no longer needed for the ships; therefore, we were taken to the beach and piled into trucks for a trip to another camp. Some members of our crew were left to pull heavy ammunition carts and field pieces over the rough terrain, but I was one of the truck passengers. The convoy started, but almost at once we came to a halt. Road blocks had been thrown up everywhere. Bridges were damaged and native huts were abandoned. Apparently the natives had evacuated the huts, expecting a battle. Our progress was very slow.

Farther along, we saw an old man lolling in the shade of a coconut tree, while women, wearing sarongs that came only to their waists beat rice. Children and dogs swarmed about them. As we proceeded, some of the natives threw rocks at us, jeering, and the children rushed to the roadside waving tiny Japanese flags. We were extremely surprised to see the natives had gone over to the enemy. Suddenly, a small American flag was thrust out from behind a hut and waved boldly in view of the guards. There were angry words and the convoy stopped while they scrambled after the old man waving the flag. They beat him about the head and shoulders with fists and rifles and confiscated the flag. It was a game after that, watching for the flag; it gave us more hope than they knew. Sometimes it appeared briefly in a brown hand high above a clump of shrubbery, or around the bough of a tree; then, as suddenly as it came it disappeared. Zealous guards searched frantically for the offender, but sometimes they were unable to detect him and vented their wrath by shouting curses at a group of apparently innocent natives. The guards were ill-trained for their jobs and behaved in a primitive fashion, their faces contorted by rage. Their malevolence seemed to extend far beyond what a person might expect under the circumstances. They lacked what we in America called "common decency."

It took four hours for us to complete the relatively short trip to Serang, on the northeastern coast of Java, where we were driven slowly through the town between rows of more jeering natives. We stopped in front of an old theater enclosed by a high stone wall. Here we were unloaded, counted and pushed inside. It was very dark and, after riding in the bright sunshine, it took me several seconds to adjust my eyes to the gloom. When I finally achieved this, I could scarcely believe what I saw. Seated on the concrete floor—most of them naked except for a scrap of clothing, unshaven, filthy beyond belief, hollow-eyed and packed together like sardines in a can—were more than 1,500 white men. The guard, using his boot, kicked a space for us on the floor. Swinging his rifle butt, he enlarged this to accommodate us, sitting, but just barely. He told us to "sit at attention, make no noise and not talk." And then he left us.

Dutch, American, British and Australian prisoners were seated on the concrete, or squatting on their haunches. There was no light, except that given by the three doors, but I could see at once that the place was unspeakably filthy. Lying all about on the dirty floor were the sick and wounded, some of whom appeared to be critically ill. Droves of flies buzzed about their open, unbandaged wounds, in spite of the efforts of their friends to keep them off.

On the balcony a number of guards, dressed in camouflage, with field packs beside them, sat with machine guns trained on the prisoners. It was obvious that the enemy had been ill-prepared for the great number of prisoners. These men were field troops being used for guard duty.

The high stone wall cut off any breeze that might have cooled the theater, the hundreds of bodies adding their heat to the already tropical atmosphere. The men were miserable from the tropical heat and the stifling, nauseating stench from the latrine located six feet outside the wall of the building.

Despite the order to maintain silence, some of the prisoners beside us whispered that which we needed no one to tell us: that we had arrived in Hell. Many of the men were ill from malaria, burns, jaundice, dysentery and wounds of all description. They had had no medical attention and no medicines of any type. Water was issued, a pint to each man, every 24 hours. There were no work details.

Food, consisting of usually sour, frequently wormy, boiled rice, was issued once or twice daily, with an occasional portion of cooked weeds. Tea, served in pails, came à la spiders, cockroaches and a variety of debris.

We were told that some of the men from the ships who had managed to get ashore, had been captured by the natives and turned over to the enemy. The Japs had beaten them mercilessly. Others had been beaten by the natives and at least two had been beheaded by the Parangs of the Sulanese. A number of men had died in the water from Jap torpedoes and shells that had exploded against the sides of the ships. Some had been shot by the enemy and still others had been carried out to sea by the treacherous currents off the Java coast. Altogether only 330 men from the *Perth* and 350 from the *Houston* had survived and many of these were very ill. The remaining prisoners in the theater were Dutch or British.

The high stone wall around the theater was topped by broken glass and spikes. Beyond this, barbed wire was arranged in such a fashion that it would be most discouraging to anyone intent upon making an escape.

The latrine, I soon discovered, was an open pit, only partly covered by boards. This was the only sanitary facility for a total of almost 2,000 men. I helped carry one of the dysentery patients to the latrine and, on the return trip, met the men who had been left at the beach to pull the heavy enemy equipment. Blood ran from their feet and they were on the verge of collapse from the hot sun and lack of nourishment of any kind.

For the evening meal a small quantity of half-cooked rice was issued. I found it was very dirty and contained a number of small pieces of gravel. Some of the men bit down on these before they noticed them, doing considerable damage to their teeth. Dusk fell and the mosquitoes came in droves. I lay down on the floor with no covering. There wasn't even a coconut tree to cut down here.

After a restless night, during which I took turns with the other men in caring for the sick, morning arrived, accompanied by another issue of the bad rice. This time, it was sour and was issued with a small amount of cooked seaweed. Almost at once the theater became very hot, the flies returned and the sick continued to moan. In the clearer light of day, I saw that the wounds, many of which were very bad, had no dressings and almost all of them were badly infected. Some of the men had been horribly burned, others had deep shrapnel wounds and many had fractured bones. An American marine was desperately ill with malaria and acute jaundice, but no treatment was given him except what his fellow prisoners could offer.

Some of us complained to the guards and an American doctor was permitted to see the sick. His efforts were rendered almost useless by the lack of medical equipment; the marine grew worse as the day progressed. On the morning of the third day he died. The space was not sufficient for everyone to lie down inside, therefore many slept outside. Those who remained had only enough room to sleep on their sides. When one man turned over, 20 others were forced to follow suit. The concrete bit into our almost bare hip bones and our nights of rest were hardly that.

"Seeing all of these young, healthy fellows as ill as they are and knowing you could save most of them if only you had a few basic medicines … it's murder, pure and simple murder," groaned a doctor.

Gordon and I took turns caring for Short during the night. He became delirious and called "Mother! Mother!" several times. Gordon and I agreed it was a blessing that his mother could not see him under these conditions.

Chuck Satterlee could enliven a funeral procession with two sentences and he never failed to keep us awake when he was in view. During the heaviest of the rain, when few of us were sleeping and dawn was trying to break, we heard a commotion. I raised my head to see Chuck, furious as usual, making his way toward us. He wore nothing but a pair of crumpled, dirty shorts and for some reason was clawing on the hair on his chest hard enough to almost uproot it.

"Good God Almighty, a #$%^& maggot crawled onto my chest! Right here!"

"That was a mighty brave maggot," I said.

"Who in the hell do these goggle-eyed bastards think they are throwing us into a shit hole like this?" He choked on his indignation but continued to thump his chest with a stubby forefinger, his bright blue eyes afire with fury. "Really," he went on, "I wish I had me a handful of red hot peppers. I'd sure as hell stick them up their asses, gun or no gun."

The old guard, whose name was Nasaki, roused himself enough to tell Chuck he must not make a disturbance.

"WHAT?" roared Chuck, looking for all the world as though he intended to slug the guard until Gordon told him that this was the old man who had brought the doctor for Short and Chuck's hackles began to fall.

"*Dommi-dommi!* Beat *beokee!* Beat sick man!" warned Nasaki, nodding toward the 20 or 30 other guards scattered about among the prisoners, training their machine guns on us.

"I can't take this damned captivity," Chuck complained, wearily, rubbing his hands over his face. "What kind of creatures are these Japs? Animals, huh? All these sick guys and not even a chancre mechanic to take care of them! And the food! Who in the hell can eat the food? There's not even enough of it to keep a piss ant alive. Like, look at the dysentery jerks. They sleep on the latrine because they are too weak to make it to the head!"

When breakfast, consisting of a small quantity of sour rice and seaweed arrived, we made no attempt to feed it to Short, who looked ghastly in the daylight. Even the whites of his eyes were lemon-colored and he was burning with fever. We left Gordon to care for his needs and give him a small ration of water and went into the yard where we used pebbles to kill five small, sparrow-like birds, built a fire and cooked them on pieces of tin found in the yard.

While we were cooking them, Johnny Sayre, another marine from our ship, came out of the theater and told us he had been caring for some of the sick. This included a marine named Bob McCann, who had a badly infected leg and an Aussie with a broken shoulder and severe burns on his legs. He brought down two more small birds and when they were all cooked we gave them to Short, McCann and the Aussies.

Despite our efforts, Short became worse and, on the following morning, succumbed to his disease. Just before he died, he called us about him and, raising a weak hand, waved it feebly about the room. "I am sorry, so sorry fellows." We thought he meant he was sorry to die, but after a few more efforts to make himself heard, we finally got the gist of his message. He was sorry we had not gone down with the ship and had to live under these conditions. "I hoped you hadn't made it!" he whispered, and with that, he turned his head to one side and dropped off into a sleep from which he never awakened.

Gordon, Sayre, Chuck and several others from the *Houston* had been fortunate enough to sustain no injuries. We busied ourselves trying to make life more pleasant for the ill. On the day after Short died, however, I came down with dysentery, and was too ill to know or care what was happening around me. By the following night, there was a tropical downpour causing maggots to crawl out of the latrine and over the bodies of the sick. Those of us with dysentery slept on the boards over the latrine with the rain pelting on us. It was small wonder that many of them contracted pneumonia.

Chuck and Gordon took turns caring for my needs and by the end of the second week I was able to sit up once more. On the afternoon of this day, a small, vicious-looking Jap officer strode into the building. We were told to stand at attention. I was able to do this with the assistance of Chuck and Gordon, but for some of the men, it was quite impossible, particularly since many had severe leg wounds and one man near us had two broken legs. It was obvious that the officer was desperately anxious to use his pistol on some of us. We were determined to see that we did not provoke him.

The officious little man walked over to three ill men, sitting on the concrete and slapped each of them in the face, spewing Japanese invective at everyone. We learned some of the words and others were translated for us by the old Jap guard whose heart, as I mentioned before, never seemed to be in what he was doing. On every occasion he could, without incurring the wrath of his superiors, he talked to us and helped us in small ways.

We sat quietly, as though our lives depended on our not making a motion, which in reality it did. Finally, the obnoxious officer strode from the theater, obviously disappointed that he had been unable to provoke some show of violence. No doubt there was a limit to how long he could bear the stench from the latrine pit.

After he had gone Chuck asked Nasaki to give us a rundown on what the officer had said. We learned a handful of new words we had not known before and Chuck, looking puzzled and indignant at the same time, told Nasaki: "After the war is over and you see him again, and he can't shoot us, give him a message for me. Tell him that we feel the same way about him. Only, we don't go around smacking sick people to show how big and strong we are. I'd say that after the war I would beat him up, but the guy is sick. He don't need a beating. He needs a headshrinker, understand? He's squirrely!" Chuck made some grotesque gesticulations to show the old man what his feelings were about the mental state of the offensive officer. Nasaki nodded and looked sad. I felt sure he was really quite unhappy with his present role and very homesick, as we all were.

We were not only homesick, but we had no illusions about our chances of survival under the conditions existing in the theater.

"Jim," said Gordon, seriously, "three men died while you were very ill. We must think of something, some way, to get out of this atmosphere. You'll be able to walk in a few days and if we could get some fresh air and exercise we would stand a better chance."

"I can't think very well," I answered. "Maybe if I had a shower I might be able to think of something. A revolt is hardly feasible under the circumstances. You might say the inmates are not exactly in prime condition."

"What I had in mind," Gordon continued, ignoring my attempt at levity, "is a swim. Nasaki has taken a shine to you and when you were ill he kept hovering around, afraid you would die. He got the doctor when you asked. Why not ask him if we could take a swim in the river where they get the water for cooking?"

The Spirit moved the flesh. The thought of a swim, or in my case, a chance to wash and to get out the stench that permeated everything in the theater gave strength to my wobbly legs. Without another word, I struggled to my feet and, with Gordon's help, went to see Nasaki, who guarded one of the doors not far from us.

Once more, he went to consult a superior and, once more, he returned with a positive answer. We could go! Our reaction at being allowed out of the dark, smelly prison was a happiness bordering on hysteria. Every man who was not in a coma made an attempt. Even those like McCann, who had one broken leg, made the trek assisted by those who had two good legs.

No matter how long I live, and how many delights I enjoy, I shall count the joy of splashing the cool water on my hot, dirty skin, and—even as my strength seemed to surge back—immersing my whole body in the cool wetness, one of the most pleasant experiences of my life.

The fact that large pieces of sewage floated in the creek from which we knew they obtained water for our tea and drinks would have appalled us before our capture. I gathered that the creek was the means of disposing of the town's sewage, but after two weeks in the Java heat without a bath, it took more than a trifle like this to dampen our enthusiasm.

We returned to the prison much refreshed and had scarcely settled ourselves when a Jap officer, holding his pistol in front of him and obviously very frightened, walked into the theater. He kicked and slapped at several of the prisoners near him, but, unlike his predecessors, the hand that held the gun shook. This did nothing to help us feel more comfortable; quite the reverse. Nasaki, who had accompanied us on the trip to the creek, was nearby and I whispered to him, asking why the officer was being brutal when we were standing at attention as best we could and trying to follow the instructions given us.

"Melicans no bow. Makee angry," he returned, quietly.

Chuck, Marv, Gordon and I started bowing and saluting as though we were deeply honored to have him there, and soon everyone in the theater who was able was following suit. This obviously gave him much "face" before the guards and he beamed at us. Still holding his pistol in front of him, but with the tremor in his hand less noticeable, he began to speak.

"You are our first prisoners of war. You are a great burden to us. Your guards are front line troops badly needed in the field." They are standing double watches. They are not trained in handling prisoners."

"You better believe it!" whispered Chuck.

"Can you tell us what happened to the Dutch?" asked Sergeant Quarles, a marine from the *Houston*.

The question did not annoy the Jap, but the answer was a stunning blow to us. "They, too, must be guarded," he explained. "We have forty thousand Dutch and a hundred thousand natives who have surrendered. We must set up camps all over Java. Your conditions will improve. It is hard for us."

The impact of his words struck us hard. We had pinned all our hopes on an early release when the Dutch began a counteroffensive.

"There," said McCann, as the officer walked out, "go my hopes for my being home at Easter." He had spoken for all of us. We had scarcely realized there could be an alternative to short captivity. The depression that settled over all of us was deep and almost tangible. We had all learned to talk in very low voices and for hours the theater buzzed with conversation. I am afraid there were few kind words for the Dutch Allies, but we were in possession of only a small segment of what had happened on the island. This was the worse aspect of the situation. We were in almost total ignorance of the overall picture of the war. Why, we wondered, did it take the Allies forever to fight back?

Our consternation and concern were sufficiently great to prevent much change in our mood when the Japs announced that we would be given extra rations. We had already received our daily ration of sour rice and we could not imagine what they had in mind. We were not too surprised when the food did not materialize and we went to bed hungry, as usual. At 0200 we were awakened and told our extra ration was ready. Each of us was given a small ball of uncooked dough dipped in sweetened water. We were unable to eat it despite our hunger, but hoarded it for baking when dawn arrived.

If we were to be interred for an indefinite time, it was imperative that we become resourceful. After trying to fall asleep again, we were roused by Johnny Sayre, who had had a brainstorm. He recalled that his mother had sometimes made a delicious chicken pie. He suggested the dough be used for this purpose. Chuck promptly told him to drop dead, but this in no way diminished his enthusiasm for the idea.

"Where in the hell will you get the damn chicken?" asked Chuck.

"Will you can the gab and let us go to sleep?"

"Aha!" Johnny replied undaunted. "Wait until that rooster jumps up on the fence this morning to crow. I'll pretend I'm going to the latrine pit. Savvy?"

Not only did we savvy, but four of us stayed awake the rest of the night to make sure that Johnny did not oversleep. McCann made some comment about a bird in the hand and went to sleep. Four hours later, every prisoner in the theater who could swallow had one bite of scorched, but delicious rooster pie.

Following the chicken pie incident, some of the Aussies accused the Texans of having more money than most of the prisoners and therefore being in a better position to survive.

"That's not it at all," Johnny returned. "We just know how to make a little go a long way. My aunt brought my brother and me up and every single Sunday of my life I had to go out in the chicken yard with my brother and catch a chicken or two before church. Sometimes we could sneak up on them, but as likely as not, we had to run them down. It's experience that counts every time."

"Goethe said that ignorance in action is one of the most frightful things in the world," murmured one of the Aussie journalists, "but I would surely be ignorant if it came to being able to catch a rooster."

"It wasn't usually a rooster, 'cause roosters are tough, and they have other functions that are more important than making chicken pies. Usually it was an old, fat hen for pie or dumplins. My aunt would warn them ahead of time. She'd say, 'Now I'll give you till Sunday to lay an egg and if you don't, into the pot you go!' Could she ever cook chicken and dumplins! Man alive!" Johnny licked his lips and looked up at the dark ceiling.

Chuck, gritting his teeth, swung threateningly at Johnny. "I missed that time, but if you don't shut your trap about food, I'll kill ya, so help me!"

The taste of chicken spurred us to more resourceful tactics. We decided that since some of us had watches, rings and a little money, we might be able to trade with the natives if we were in a position to contact them. I asked Nasaki if there were a chance that we might be able to help with work details. He left us to make an inquiry.

The Japanese major had talked to us on March 26. By April, more prisoners had arrived and the food had not improved. Men grew worse and many died. Nasaki returned with the information that all able-bodied men could help unload ships. Out of almost 2,000 men we could find only a hundred able to work. Many were not wounded, but were too weak to walk to a work detail. Since we were in a town and our worn shorts had long ago become tattered rags, there was a problem about how to cover our bodies. The Japs solved this problem very nicely by issuing Dutch uniforms to us.

My uniform was meant for a much smaller man. I could get the trousers on, but the bottoms of the legs came only to the middle of my calves. The coat was useless, but I kept it, hoping to trade it for food.

Our crew, when dressed, was the most ludicrous-looking group upon whom anyone had ever set eyes. All of us had beards, hollow eyes, spindly legs and haircuts straight out of a hobo camp. Our clothing covered us in spots and either draped us or was skin tight. Morale was something else again. We were the most cheerful of men. Quips and comments were bandied about in a fashion we had not seen much of in the past few weeks, more like the cheerful banter of the olden days.

If we were to unload ships, that meant food. Our cheer was briefly changed to gloom when we discovered that the ships had little in the way of food. Beer, saki, and sugar were the only items that might be labeled as food but there were other things we could trade. The natives seemed interested in everything. We had a field day exchanging Jap rifles, pieces of equipment, and everything that was moveable that we could trade on the sly for food. This trading and the food obtained literally made the difference between life and death for many of us.

We had learned the importance of taking advantage of every opportunity. Things that were of little use to one prisoner were considered important to others. Nothing was allowed to go to waste and we smuggled everything we could manage. This was never too much, but even a crust was welcomed by these starving men. It was for me a jolting experience, however, to have a grown man burst into tears because I brought him a banana.

Having been brought up on a ranch, the thought of having too little to eat was never, in my life, a consideration. We had an abundant supply and enough to give away. Now, it was almost the only consideration. If we did not eat we would surely die and the prospect of dying at the age of 19 was not appealing.

I went out on details for six days before my dysentery returned and I was unable to walk. I could only wait for the others to return with some morsel to add to our sorely deficient diet. I kept McCann company. We tried discussing the food our mothers would be giving us if we were home in our present physical condition, but this soon became too depressing. We found talking to prisoners who were in worse condition than we were to be about the only thing that took our minds off of our troubles. Some of them were much older than us and in worse shape because of this. As one man put it, "getting old comes when the days drag and the years fly, but in this place the whole process is accelerated."

We waited anxiously for Marv, Gordon, Chuck and Johnny to return from the work detail. They not only brought us food, but news of sabotage and odds and ends of information. Some of it was only rumor, but it was the only news we had. Marv Miller, who enjoyed a practical joke when he was the one playing it, found his friends not in a receptive mood under these conditions. Failing with them, he recounted to us how the Japs had become his favorite target for the jokes. One day he found a piece of resin in one of the packages he was transporting and put it into the gasoline barrels. Sugar in the gasoline was an old standby by now and removing tiny, vital pieces of machinery and either dropping them overboard or into shrubbery gave him solace after the poor reception he received from us.

On April 14, John brought us the first news worthy of the name. We were moving to Batavia.

"Just another rumor," I suggested.

"Not this one. A Jap officer told us," John shot back, promptly.

We considered this thoughtfully. Batavia was a much larger city. That meant more opportunities would be available for trading.

"The bastards are taking us out to shoot us," said Chuck, darkly. "They want their rotten garbage for themselves."

John drew himself up to his full six-foot-three-inch height and looked down on Chuck with mock disapproval. "Listen, son," he growled at Chuck, "didn't you ever hear of esprit de corp?"

Chuck looked puzzled.

"It's a fancy word for morale, just as derrière is a fancy word for backside. French, that is," offered Marv, helpfully.

"Can you tell me what the hell that's got to do with getting lead poisoning from the Japs?" asked Chuck, genuinely annoyed.

"Not a thing," retorted John. "Neither word is important if you are getting shot by the Japs. There is a point, though; you see a lot of these guys already depressed enough. Your talk doesn't bother us 'cause we know you are older and have a right to be more pessimistic. You've seen a lot of the world. Maybe we ought to be pessimistic, but don't have enough sense to be. Just try to be less ... what's the word I want?" asked John.

"Dolorous," said the Aussie journalist.

"Dolorous," John repeated.

"The Jap lieutenant told us," put in Gordon, "that twenty guys with dysentery are leaving tomorrow for Batavia."

"I don't know whether I'm in that category or not." This came from McCann.

We quickly assured him that everyone in the camp was in that category and told him not to worry about his qualifications.

"Don't look so sad, Chuck," said Marv, "about our not getting shot. I heard they planned to shoot us, fellah, but so many guys are already dying that they decided to go along with their present scheme of starving us to death and save all of that good lead."

Suddenly McCann pointed out that there would be Dutch women in Batavia and, looking at me, asked if I planned to wear the beautiful "High-water Willy" outfit I wore on work details.

This comment sent me into action and, borrowing a needle and some thread, and begging a piece of cloth here and there, I sat down and sewed for two hours until I had a pair of trousers that reached my ankles. It is true that they were not all of the same material, much less of the same color, but, trousers I had.

CHAPTER 8

Batavia, Java: You Can Take the Man Out of Texas

On the morning of April 17, I was one of the 20 patients crowded into the truck for the trip to Batavia. With usual Jap efficiency, it took three days from the date of the announced time of departure to the actual day we left.

I had lain awake the night before the trip worrying about every triviality an overwrought imagination is capable of concocting. I feared my friends and I would be separated for the duration of the war. I was apprehensive that the new camp might prove worse than Serang. Perhaps, I thought, we were being taken to a pest house to die. Did the Japs plan to abandon us along the way, knowing we were too ill to help ourselves? I knew the last thought was foolish. We could die in the theater. Someone did, almost daily

When I reached the truck I was doubtful that I had the strength to heave myself onto it. Certainly, I could not ask one of the other prisoners who were in the same shape or worse to help me. I made a mighty effort, but it took all of my reserve energy and drained the last ounce of my strength. I held on to the sides of the truck with my heart pounding violently against my ribs.

We were a sorry-looking crew. Gaunt, bearded, hollow-eyed, worried, and dressed in patched Dutch uniforms, we could have only looked to be a group of near-dead with only enough life left in us to take a last ride. Our own appearance and the way we felt were depressing enough, but when we began to pass the native huts along the road, gloom spread in a heavy cloud. The same natives who had looked at us with hostility or indifference on the trip to the theater now stood behind huts or shrubbery and wept as they waved to us.

Twice in a short space of road, a native, one a man, another a woman, boldly stepped out waving an American flag at us. These instances of pro-American feeling brought instant reprisals from the guards, who rained blows with rifle butts down upon their heads. The woman left bleeding by the roadside raised her head and spat defiantly at the oppressors. This daring action from the natives gave us a new lease on life. We suddenly decided we had no time to die. We must get well and reward their loyalty, and teach the enemy a lesson in the bargain. Each of us wanted to have a hand in both.

There were other cheering signs of native resistance. The enemy had recently repaired bridges that had been sabotaged by the Dutch or the natives. As we neared some of these, we found every kind of road block in the way of the truck. The reaction of the Japs to this show of disaffection was all out of proportion to what you might expect. Instead of removing the obstacles and proceeding along the road, the guards attacked the road blocks with their rifles, fists, and even kicked them spitefully with their boots. They were infuriated, behaving much like small, spoiled boys who had been frustrated at play. When the logs and timber and various odds and ends had been removed they still stomped about the roadway, their faces distorted with fury, shaking their fists at the shrubbery. We were a bit anxious for the truck to proceed, since we only had one pail for a latrine and 20 dysentery patients to share it. A washtub would have been more appropriate, except that there would have been no room for it in the corner of the truck.

We arrived in Batavia by mid-afternoon. We were ravenous, having had no food since before dawn. Brown, yellow, white and black men were going about their activities, largely ignoring our strange crew. We were taken to the center of town and directed to get off the truck and march to a huge camp, surrounded on three sides by a high stone wall, and on the fourth, with barbed wire. My knees buckled twice between leaving the truck and arriving at the door of the hospital hut to which we were herded, but I made it inside the doorless cubicle indicated by the guard. I fell across an empty makeshift bed that made me think for a moment that I must be occupying the Jap commandant's sack. Compared to the cement floor at Serang, it felt heavenly.

I realized that there were two other patients in the room, Mike Sullivan and George Sampson, both fellow Texans, but it was all I could do to breathe after the exertion of the walk from the truck.

"Well, Mike," said George, with a soft, Texas drawl, "the Japs have sent us a scarecrow. That one's not from Texas 'cause ours have more to them than that."

"That's not a scarecrow, George; it walked in here. It's from some kind of army, but did you ever see a uniform like that one? All those colors? Looks like Joseph's coat!"

"Well, he didn't make it a minute too soon. He's all tuckered out. Some critters live back in the hills and eat nothin' but poke salad. Could be that kind. Hey, Johnson! Look what the monsoon blew in!"

Johnson, a tall, red-haired corpsman, appeared at my feet, took one look at me and whistled, "Kee-eerist! Another old one with the shits." Let me get him some chow while he's still able to hold a spoon." He disappeared, to appear with the nearest thing to a full meal that I had seen since leaving the ship. I wolfed it down, fearing it was either a dream, or not meant for me.

The fellows continued their cheerful banter. When the corpsman returned for the tray not one crumb of the meal remained.

"What's the matter with your appetite, son? Don't you like our cuisine? I'll send that lousy chef in here at once! Doc will get you some vitamin pills, too. When you came in, you looked like a string. Now, you look better. Maybe like a string with a knot tied in it. Good God, what did they feed you guys?"

"Johnson!" roared Mike, "If I've told you once, I've told you a thousand times not to use the Lord's name in vain! Every time you say something like that, I see my old man's black snake whip and the woodshed. Call on somebody that knows you."

"I know all about your old man's black snake whip. So, spare me, Jack. I apologize. Next time I'll say good conscience! OK?"

"OK!"

As my strength surged back after the good meal, I began to pepper them with questions.

"It could only be better than where you came from," said Mike. "We have about 2,000 men. The first to arrive were the Aussies who set up the camp. We have doctors, corpsmen, and some food. We get a lot more by smuggling—that's the way we get most of the medicine, too."

"The Dutch women bring a lot of things," George put in, "Soap, pills, food and all kinds of stuff. The Japs beat them if they catch them. If a guard ever starts to beat one, don't watch. He'll beat her as long as you look at him. Turn your back, then the beating won't last as long."

"The Japs enjoy watching us get mad enough to burst a blood vessel, because they are beating a woman and we can't do anything about it. I hope the day never comes when I'm so low down mean that I'll beat a woman." Mike brought his right fist down sharply in the palm of his left hand.

"Simmer down, sonny," George cautioned. "When the Japs finally do manage to starve us to death that won't be until all the bugs and grass and dirt is gone. I'll have a talk with St. Peter and ask him to put a special handful of stars in the crowns of those Dutch women. They've earned 'em."

It was almost immediately apparent to me that survival depended upon smuggling. There were many small cliques and each member of a group provided for himself and helped procure items for those in his circle who were hospitalized or incapacitated. I was in the latter category for a shorter time than one might imagine. The doctors, who made rounds in a group daily, ordered charcoal, bismuth, and nourishing food. There was a Dutch, an English and an American doctor, and four days after my arrival, they had me walking about the compound. My heart no longer beat against my ribs like jungle drums each time I took a step. I was not, however, exactly filled with vigor.

The difference between Serang's theater and the camp at Batavia was incomparable. Here there were concrete barracks with raised wooden roofs, a modern cookhouse with steam, a bath-house and a sewer. The prisoners were grouped according to nationality and each group provided a cook. An officer was in charge of enlisted men and he in turn was responsible to a superior.

My progress was fast and by April 24 I was permitted to move into a barracks. I missed Gordon, McCann, Sayre, and the others and thought constantly how much better for them it would be at this camp.

On the following morning I was returning from the bath-house when a truckload of prisoners arrived from Serang. The first man removed from the truck was a stretcher case: Bob McCann. My joy at seeing him instantly changed to a feeling of alarm and concern when I saw the condition of his leg. It was enormously swollen and bright red streaks had started to move upward toward his groin.

"Guess they'll have to amputate," he said, morosely. He was unshaven, hollow-cheeked, and his face bore the unmistakable marks of having endured intense pain. Except for the greatly swollen leg, he was very emaciated.

I lost no time in informing him about the immeasurably better conditions at Batavia "Bicycle Camp," as it had been named, and he furnished me the news that Gordon, Marv, Chuck and John were scheduled to arrive within a few days.

After he was settled in a hospital hut and the corpsman had brought him the first decent meal he had had in ten weeks, I left him to enjoy it in peace and went to help some of the others build an oven.

One of the things we yearned for most in prison camp was home-baked bread. In Texas families, hot, home-baked bread was commonplace. We took it for granted, just as we Americans take so many things for granted until we are without them, or are deprived of their benefits. We had talked about it nostalgically more times than we could count, but that was as far as it went. As I grew stronger, I began to help the cooks with meals. After three days of this, several of us decided we needed only an oven to produce our much-loved bread. We set about building one, amid the jeers of our fellow prisoners, including McCann. After a few days of decent food, being shaved by a corpsman, having the doctors clean and pour sulpha into his wound, the red streaks had totally disappeared and, with no talk of amputation, McCann was ready to join our committee.

It took us three days to build the oven, and when it was finished everyone cheered. At last we had an oven ... but nothing to bake! While we were stewing over this problem and trying to figure out a way of obtaining the necessary ingredients for bread, trucks arrived with more prisoners from Serang. Marv, Gordon, Chuck and John were in this group. They looked so depressed and altogether spiritless that I knew we must do something to revive their sagging interest in life.

"We are going to have some hot biscuits for breakfast," I told them, trying not to look at the bones jutting through their dreadfully thin flesh.

Chuck looked at me with dull eyes, his broad shoulders slumped, but summoned enough energy to raise a right forefinger and point it at me defiantly. "Yeah," he croaked, "then we'll grow some hair on an egg!"

Leaving them to get some rest and a decent meal—decent compared to what they were accustomed to—Mike Sullivan and I went to beg some flour from the Japs. Under the supervision of the guards, we carried saltwater in five-gallon cans and boiled it down to get salt. We made a large, flat cake from the two ingredients and baked it. The end result tasted more like my mother's cooking than anything I had had since leaving Texas, although she would not have recognized it.

Everyone in our group had hot bread for dinner. We had no butter, no jam, and the "bread" would not have been recognized as such by any self-respecting Southern mom, but to us it was a bit of home. It started us reminiscing about the "cuisine" we had had at various times before our imprisonment, particularly some of the more delicious concoctions of our respective mothers, aunts and grandmothers.

Talk about home and the luscious meals thoroughly depressed us and we sought to lift the mood by singing, "The Yellow Rose of Texas," in loud voices, which promptly brought the guards. We expected a beating, but, to our astonishment, they did not lash out with their usual blows and Japanese profanity: they stood dumbfounded to see people not only singing, but clapping their hands while living under these conditions.

Having been given an inch, we promptly took a mile and swung into "Deep in the Heart of Texas," in which we not only clapped our hands, but stomped our feet. When we finished morale had never been higher since our capture. I went to bed and dreamed that my mother was roasting a turkey, that my steady girlfriend, Alicia, was helping with the dinner and that all of the family was gathered about my home in a cheerful, peacetime mood. There was one jarring note: a Japanese guard kept stepping in and out of the French door off the dining room singing "The Yellow Rose of Texas," in a horrible, high-pitched singsong voice. Even in my dreams I could not escape them.

The guards at Batavia Bicycle Camp were quite strict. As usual, I learned this the hard way. On the evening following the singing session, after having spent the day putting finishing touches on the oven, I was exhausted. After finishing my evening meal, I went into the barracks and sat down on my bed. My back was toward the door and I did not see the tiny Jap guard approaching. I was startled when he appeared very abruptly before me and shrieked "*Kiwotsuke!*" His face was suffused with anger.

I stood at attention, towering over him. This was the same as pouring kerosene over a fire. He furiously drew himself up to his full height, which must have been all of 4'11" and tried to puff out his chest. I remembered the fable of the frog who puffed himself full of air until he exploded; the little guard looked as though he might do just that. He glowered ferociously up at me then, jerking his rifle at his shoulder, pointed it at me, menacingly.

I had not been made aware of the pettiness of the guards in the camp and, for a short interval, I thought this was a case of mistaken identity. Just the same, I was quite scared as he motioned for me to walk ahead of him out of the barracks. I had heard too much about trigger-happy guards to feel otherwise.

Once outside, he pointed to a shallow ditch that ran the length of the porch and indicated that I should stand in it. It looked too shallow for a grave, but I knew such a trivial consideration would not prevent his shooting me.

I planted my feet firmly in the ditch and began to say my prayers. The Jap guard stationed himself directly opposite of me on the porch, which made him two inches taller than his victim.

He then proceeded to slap me across the face three times. He then drew his right fist back and gave me a resounding sock on the jaw. My knees, weak from my past illness, buckled very slightly. I waited to see what was next in store, but he drew back, triumph written on his face. He showed no desire to continue the one-sided fight. His general attitude seemed to say: "Well, now you know who is in charge here!" He strode off, jauntily, as though he had just won the war single-handedly.

After this incident I was more attentive when I saw the guards coming and tried to keep on the lookout for them. They strolled in pairs throughout the camp, bearing rifles at least six inches longer than they were. Their uniforms were certainly not uniforms in appearance, being grey, tan, green, brown and countless variations of these shades. Most of them were far too large.

I soon learned that they gave beatings for a series of offenses: smiling, not smiling, singing or whistling American songs, misunderstanding an order given in Japanese, making a mistake in counting off at morning *tenko*, bathing outside of the regular hours allotted for this, trading with the natives and not bowing or saluting the moment that they caught sight of you, or for no reason, whatever.

We might have endured our captivity with less frustration had the Japs been able to command our respect. Often their ludicrous appearance and outrageous behavior made it impossible for us to avoid laughing outright, which brought instant reprisals. They behaved very much as small boys having tantrums, and each time they were thwarted in the least way, reacted violently with an emotional explosion.

They had a habit of appearing at the most inconvenient times and shouting for us to stand at attention. On one such occasion, Chuck was taking his bath. We took baths by pouring water over our bodies with a tin cup, dipping from a pail. It was a tedious way to take a bath and Chuck was not known for his patience. On this afternoon he was busily engaged in trying to perform this feat. He held a large pail of water in one hand and the tin cup in the other. Suddenly, two small guards appeared and shouted "*Kiwotsuke!*" When he saw the guards he felt this invasion of his privacy was more than any man should have to bear, and, unloosing a string of Marine Corps profanity, he stood up, shook a wet, soapy finger at them and shrieked "SCAT!" with great fury.

The tiny guards looked at him dumbfounded. This was a new word to them and they appeared to assume that it was an unspeakably vile epithet, because of the force with which it was pronounced. They did not beat him, but struck out at him spitefully with their fists then left without insisting that he stand at attention.

More prisoners continued to arrive at Batavia Camp until we had a total of 3,300 men. There were 800 Americans, most of whom were from Texas, 2,000 Australians and 500 British.

The senior Japanese officer commanding the camp was a Captain Suzuki. He was assisted by an assortment of other officers. The camp commandant was Colonel Searle of the U.S. Army. Brigadier A. S. Blackburn was the Allied C.O.

On May 15, a group of Americans arrived in camp. They were part of the 131st Field Artillery, from the 36th Division of the Texas National Guard. We received them with enormous enthusiasm. They brought news of America in general and Texas in particular. This included news of Allied losses and many stories concerning their own exploits against Japan before they were finally taken prisoner.

They had done their best to plague the Japs, and had succeeded. Taking turns walking the streets of Batavia, Magalong, and Bandong, using the same men each time, they promenaded in the different cities, leading the enemy to believe that there were many Americans in the area. They had succeeded in being a general nuisance to the enemy before they were captured.

One man, an American sergeant of Japanese descent, had flown his plane low over the enemy positions, talking to the Japanese in their native language. They lowered their guard and came out to see who the new pilot was, whereupon he had proceeded to mow them down with machine-gun fire. When captured he was asked if he was Japanese. He feigned astonishment and replied: "Me? Not me. I'm a Mexican-American."

The Japanese had not stripped these men of their money or valuables. This was unheard of among the POWs. The newcomers had with them tennis rackets, books, musical instruments, and a variety of things we'd almost forgotten existed. Most of all, they brought hope and optimism, which acted as a tonic to our flagging spirits.

The arrival of the new prisoners was not, however, an unmixed blessing. They brought with them Cyril Morgan, a captain from Queens,

New York, who caused us as much discomfort, psychologically at least, as the Japs. We hated his guts and for good reason. I had had little experience with men of Captain Morgan's type. Bob McCann described him as a "wheeler and dealer." Why he had left New York and joined the Texas National Guard, no one seemed to know. Morgan did not dispense gratuitous information about himself.

He always had a cigarette when no one else had one. I did not smoke, but many of the sick did, when they could get cigarettes. They felt the cigarettes helped appease their hunger. Morgan was plump and well-fed while the rest of us were slowly dying of starvation. He let a cigarette dangle from his lips and tried to look like a gambler from a Mississippi riverboat, displaying a patronizing attitude toward the other prisoners. He never did any work, but he always had plenty of money. It was our sad misfortune to have him for our group officer. He was supposed to intercede on our behalf with the Japs, if necessary, to buy extra food from them with money we turned over to him, and to generally look out for our welfare. It took considerable prodding to ensure that he did this.

As soon as I was able, I volunteered for a work detail and was given the job of driving a truck. The Japs kept 200 of us busy moving confiscated goods from the buildings in Batavia to the ships waiting in the harbor to take the loot to Japan. There were only ten guards assigned to us and they could not watch such a large number effectively. We proceeded to do a bit of confiscating of our own. The articles we obtained in this way were traded with the natives for money. Since we were searched going and coming from the compound, money was about the only thing easily concealed.

The money we derived from this activity was turned over to Captain Morgan as soon as we felt we had a sufficiently large sum to buy food. We waited expectantly for the rations to improve, but after two days of the usual menu of rice and eggplant preserves, we became something less than patient. John Sayre and I were on work details and had little time to investigate the problem, but Chuck and Gordon were unable to work and we asked them to do some detective work for us.

When we returned from our work details that evening, John and I went in search of them to get a report. Our "private eyes" gave us information calculated to blow the roof off of our barracks. The money that we had acquired and carefully hoarded was being put to excellent use by the officers. Their breakfast consisted of hotcakes and syrup; they enjoyed chicken for their lunch and steak for their dinner; their mid-afternoon snack consisted of hot chocolate and cookies and their dessert at lunchtime was chocolate pie, something we had seen only in our dreams for longer than we could remember

John and I went on the double to register a complaint. Our group officer was standing just outside the officers' mess, conversing with Lieutenant Shoales, a National Guard officer who could usually be found at the captain's heels, a lot like a puppy following its mother about. They listened politely, but with considerable surprise to our complaint.

"It is obvious," said Shoales, smoothly, "that you have been misinformed. We have the same food that you are issued, nothing better, nothing worse. Of course, our cooks may be a lot better than yours. You would be amazed at how good they really are." He paused for our acceptance of his explanation.

Captain Morgan, rubbing his small, black mustache with his right forefinger, seemed to surmise that this was all the explanation that we needed. "You guys are from the country, you see. Real hayseeds. You can't imagine what a Chinese cook can do with rice, for example," he added.

It took all of my self-control to keep from punching him in the nose. I was facing the door leading into the mess and, on the mess table, one of those marvelous Chinese cooks had left a large tin of Log Cabin syrup. It was bad enough for them to steal our food, but to lie about it when Chuck and Gordon had seen them eating it was too much.

"Look, John," I murmured to Sayre, nodding in the direction of the table behind the officers.

John saw the can of syrup and his eyes widened. His face became suffused with a deep red. He glared at the two officers which such fierceness that both of them swung around to see what had produced this reaction. When their eyes rested on the telltale can, they, too, had very red faces.

"Captain Morgan and Lieutenant Shoales," Johnny's tone was a cold as a Texas Northeaster in January, "I request that we all pay a visit to the C.O.!"

Consternation swept Morgan's face. "But, but, why?" he asked.

"Because," Johnny told them, unsmilingly, "he is as interested in miracles as the rest of us, and these damned miracles don't happen every day."

Shoales looked at Morgan, obviously nonplussed. The captain shrugged his shoulders, but he looked worried.

"What's he talking about?" asked Shoales.

"Well, it's like this," Johnny continued, his voice heavy with sarcasm, "when a Chinese cook can make a tin can out of rice, it's a damned miracle, and I am sure the C. O. would be very impressed."

"No! Now, that won't be necessary," Morgan began, hurriedly. "It's better that we handle our own problems. I'll investigate and find out what's going on around here. We have to remember to go through proper channels."

"I'd like to point out one aspect of this theft," I told him, succinctly. "This is no minor pilfering situation. That food was meant for the sick, at least a good share of it was and as we all know, our food is life itself here, as it is anywhere. The difference under these conditions is that all of us would like luxuries, but who wants them at the expense of another man's life?" I tried to look Morgan in the eye, but failed. No one was ever able to succeed in locking a gaze with this man.

"OK! OK!" protested Shoales, holding up his hands as though this would affect a truce. "Let's not make a production about confiscating a few rations."

"Yeah," said Morgan, "if a guy don't look out for himself, who's gonna do it for him?"

We left them in disgust. Our rations improved at once and remarkably. I felt there was a place for officers such as these, but not in the service of their country and not in charge of sick prisoners whose food they stole. I belabored the point to Gordon until he was tired of hearing about it. Seeing him give me a strange look, I resorted to whimsy and asked whether or not I was offending him by talking about his friends.

"It's not that," he returned seriously. "You know how I feel about them. Your attitude toward their punishment is what concerns me. You apparently believe that the best way to deal with rotters like this is to meet with them, individually on a dark road some night, and beat them to a sponge. Right?"

"How did you guess?" I answered.

He ignored the question and went on. "You see, I don't look at it that way. I dislike what they do as much as anyone, but I feel it is not up to me to settle things by reprisal."

"You think that people like Morgan will not walk all over you if you allow them to? Incredible!" I told him, hotly

"Of course they will. A fellow must defend his interests. That's fine, but their punishment belongs in another arena." He raised his right thumb and pointed toward the star-studded sky over Java. "It will come from up there, Jim. You can't go around hating people. Vengeance is mine, sayeth the Lord. The Japs will get theirs and the bad actors in this war will get theirs, but if you hate people it only hurts you. Look at Chuck. He hates the enemy so much he's beginning to look like an old man. Hate is destructive for the hater."

After turning this over in my mind, I realized he was right. It was true that Chuck had aged greatly during our captivity. His hatred of the Japs amounted to an obsession. He spent literally hours plotting ways to get even with the men he called his tormenters.

If there were some officers who created problems, there were others who went far beyond the call of duty in their daily activities. I thought about this after we had gone to bed that night. Commander Epstein and Lieutenant Burrows, both doctors from the *Houston*, were diligent and self-sacrificing in their services to the sick. We also had Lieutenant Blackledge of the RAF, Captain Lumkin of the U.S. Army, Captain Daniels of the British Army and Captain Goding and Colonel Eadie from Australia. We could be proud of these men.

None of us knew how long we would be alive. We were constantly aware that each day brought us closer to massive retaliation and real danger from Allied air attacks. It was a comfort to know that we had doctors. When our country started to strike back, we would no doubt need them. We had a feeling all of us were living on borrowed time ... all of us except Gordon.

Chuck was, quite unintentionally, an unending source of amusement to us. His reactions to everything he disliked in prison camp were violent. He loathed the guards and was insulted by a glance from them. He frequently told us that but for his desire to see his three year-old son, Peter, he would "wipe up the ground" with as many as possible and die happy in a last, glorious battle.

The bathing system was not the only thing that gave him a particular pain, although it was high on his list of dislikes. He did not become accustomed to it as the rest of us did, but each time he performed this chore he felt it was a personal affront. No one can deny that pouring small, tin cups of water over a body the size of his, soaping down and repeating the pouring process was no picnic. Every day we had to listen to his gripes about bathing.

Another aspect of camp life he found more inconvenient than the method of bathing was the latrine system. He swore the whole idea had been invented by a demented Samurai "hopped up on dope" or, on occasion, that it was an unnecessarily complicated process perpetuated by the Jap commandant to cause us to lose face.

The latrines were built in the form of a trough with water running through them continually. They were a puzzle to us, at first, and we clogged them at once by using paper. The guards told us quite angrily to use the water bottles provided. I will not attempt to recount some of the comments about better things to do with the bottles. There were some advantages to having guards who did not speak our language. We were supposed to hold the bottle in the left hand, directing the stream of water along the spine.

"I won't do it! Not in a thousand years!" thundered Chuck.

"Take it easy, Chuck," Johnny suggested, "you can get used to hanging if you hang long enough."

"The hell I will! I'll get the docs to give me something to bind me up for the duration before I'll do that. I guess you guys don't think they invented this just to spite us. It's insulting. That's the way their blasted minds work!"

"Simmer down, buddy," urged Gordon. "If the colonels and other top brass have to use it, we can use it. You won't be alone."

"The great leveler," laughed Bob. "Think how the brass feels about having to be forced to use these bottles."

"I heard once from a civil engineer that the greatest achievement of modern civilization is the sewer system in the States."

"I would have said it was women," Johnny insisted.

"Women are not exactly a modern achievement," Marv insisted. "Have you forgotten Eve and Cleopatra, Mary Magdalene and a few others?"

Chuck scratched his head, "Dames is as old as the hills. Dames ARE as old as the hills, I should have said, and they are all skunks. I didn't know Eve or the others, but you've ruined a perfectly good night's sleep for me. Now I'll dream about my old bag. Why'd you have to bring up a subject like that, huh? What would we do with a dame, anyway, in our condition? A hot shower and a dame would kill me."

"Don't judge all women by your experiences. My Aunt Martha is a really good Joe. She and my uncle brought my brother, Bill, and me up and they treated us better than lots of mothers treat their own kids." This from Johnny.

"Chuck is really crazy about his wife," Gordon insisted. "He is just too shy to admit it in front of us."

"Aww-w shaddup and go to sleep or I'll show all of you wise quiz kids just how crazy I am about you. All the silly yack-yack you spiel out makes a feller feel like climbing in with the Japs for sack duty."

The following day was Mother's Day. Holidays in POW camps were always miserable. This particular one was the most painful because of our situation and the obvious significance of the occasion. A great many of us were on a work detail that Sunday. As we filed out of camp, I tried to picture my mother on her way to church. On previous Mother's Days my older brother and I, along with our youngest brother, now 12, would dress in our best suits, place a red carnation in our buttonholes, and proudly escort her to the services. I never did this, but that I thanked God for the privilege. The thought that she might die while I was in prison camp was unbearable.

We passed many natives and Dutch en route to or returning from church. Finally, as the music poured out of a door of a stone church along our way, the awfulness of the situation got the best of me, and for the first time since becoming a prisoner, tears streamed down my cheeks. I tried to check them by holding my head high, but the sun shining on my face made prisms of the tears and the passersby merged into each other in blurred outlines.

CHAPTER 9

Fourth of July, 1942

I was homesick with an intensity that defied description. No doubt malnutrition played a major part in these proceedings, but there was also a heavy mixture of nostalgia tinctured with fear. A strong premonition that my life would be a short one sat heavily on my shoulders like the Old Man of the Sea. I felt sure that a long life, marriage, home and loved ones were not to be a part of my future.

The Fourth of July was miserable for a different reason. For several weeks before the holiday, we began noticing that guards meted out more severe punishment to Americans than to the British and Aussies, for identical offenses. A rumor that the enemy expected trouble from the Yanks, because we felt so strongly about our Independence Day, was not dismissed as scuttlebutt. I knew there were those, and Chuck was one, who would produce their own fireworks if any slur were cast on his country, on this of all days.

The day arrived. We were told to fall out, were paraded about the camp, and when halted told to sign an oath of allegiance to the Japanese emperor with a promise not to attempt escape but to help the enemy in every way possible in the prosecution of the war. We, of course, refused. It was announced that the lives of the men who refused to sign would not be guaranteed. We refused again. Consequently all food, water, and canteen goods were cut off for the day, enlisted men and officers were separated, and we were told to prepare for execution. We were then beaten by the guards until we looked as though we were losers in a free-for-all. We still refused to sign.

The enemy was resourceful, if heartless. Our sick were then carried out into the pitiless Java sunshine and the guards set upon them with fists and gun butts. This was too much. The C.O. sent word that duress had been amply proven and ordered us to sign. Everyone signed except four officers who were tortured and thrown into cells. They signed after a direct order from the C.O.

Immediately after our group signed, the guards strutted about in front of us, laughing, jeering, and behaving in an obnoxious fashion. It was abundantly apparent that they felt they had demeaned us, when, actually, they had demeaned themselves. "Where," I asked myself, "are the gentle Japanese widely acclaimed for their manners? Where did these barbarians get the idea that they are invincible?"

One of the officers in the Texas 131st Artillery had been grilled about the number of men in his outfit and what the intention of our government had been. When the Jap officers were told the total compliment had been six hundred, their senior officer asked in enormous wonder: "How did your country think that they could overcome the great might of His Imperial Majesty the Emperor's forces with only six hundred men? This we cannot understand!"

"You are certainly right about that," returned the officer. "We should have sent more men." This pleased the Jap immensely.

"How many should you have sent?" asked the interrogator, smiling smugly.

"Seven hundred." He was promptly returned to his quarters.

Now, watching the Bash Artist—one of the least favorite of our guards because he beat us without reason—striding up and down in front of us, swaggering and leering, we wanted nothing so much as a chance to even the score with this one.

Finally, he stalked directly beneath our noses and made a speech. "You have long felt superior to our people," he said with a smirk. "In this way you show your ignorance. The Japanese people are descendants of the gods. In the future, you will be our servants, and that is good!"

I thought of the sick who must go without food or water for the remainder of the day, of the many bashings we had received at his hands, of the bestiality and unreasonable pride of these sadistic guards, and before I could stop myself, I made a speech of my own. "May Almighty God have mercy on your soul! You are not even a man, let alone a descendant of the gods. You are a *beast!*" I spat out, furiously. I then waited for the beating I thought inevitable.

The Bash Artist understood me perfectly, but he only looked surprised. He gave me a very odd look, and, turning upon his heel, motioned to another guard. They walked away together.

★

"Oh, what's the use? What's the use!" said Gordon in a tone of such complete disgust and near despair that we all looked at him in amazement.

"That doesn't sound like cheerful Gordon, grandpappy of the whole passel," said Mike Sullivan.

I am sure the thought went through our heads that if Gordon, a constant cheering influence on all of us, had lost hope, what must become of the rest of us? Things were indeed dismal.

Marv scratched the spot on top of his sunburned head where the tow-colored hair refused to protect his scalp. "Cheer up, you characters. I heard that two Aussies have radios hidden in the camp and I heard for a fact that the Allies will be standing right on this spot in three months' time."

There it was again. Three months. A longer period we could not endure and, in fact, even refused to try to visualize, but three months, if we lived, was only THREE MONTHS! This never failed to cheer us. Radios were something else again. Men were killed if they were found, but when your life depends upon it, you can secrete things in unthought-of places. The radios, we later learned, we disassembled and parts dispersed among many prisoners. When possible, the tiny pieces came back together like magic and the precious news was garnered by a few while countless others stood on lookout to protect them against the enemy.

A brown-out was ordered in Batavia. The Japs were becoming jittery about something. A hundred enemy planes flew back and forth and we had to undergo countless air raid drills for four days. It was a pleasure, despite the fact that the drills were held both night and day. We learned from the radio that no effective measures against the Japs were expected for 12 months, but we refused to believe it.

There was a wide variation in the talent and education of the large group of men in Batavia Bicycle Camp. Some of the prisoners could scarcely write their names, while others boasted several degrees. We tried to take advantage of this opportunity to learn about the economic, political, and religious theories held by men of widely different nationalities. We also made a successful attempt to utilize the various talents represented by the prisoners. We listened to lectures on every subject imaginable, from sheep-herding in Australia, to the climate in Great Britain. We held art exhibitions and large concerts.

Johnny Sayre had sung professionally in the States. He was often asked to sing to the P.O.W.s. Tex McFarland, Gordon, Bob, Marv and I helped produce plays. There were a number of these, one of which was *Mexican Fandango*. Chuck and Mike helped a crew backstage with lighting and props and Chuck performed a dance that brought the house down. Wearing a white chiffon dress and a scarlet sash, borrowed from a Dutch woman who brought us soap, he performed what he called "the Floozy Shuffle." He wore the sash wrapped about his head. Paid entertainment could not have been more downright hilarious.

There were other amusing plays. *Nellie, Nellie with the Rice Belly* was a favorite skit by "Doc" Clark, an Aussie comedian. Our own Bob Martin grew a beard and posed as Nostradamus, making a very popular diversion. Fred Quick, who had also sung professionally in the States, crooned popular songs; "Fugle Horn Freddy," a Dutchman, "gave out" with his trumpet, and "Poodles" Norley of the *Perth* did female impersonations.

One of the highlights of the concert was a sign that had been made from a screen. When the lights went out, in the shed where we held the performances, lighting had been arranged to create a makeshift neon sign. Since the only tobacco obtainable in the camp was a native weed called "wog," the sign blinked on and off with the announcement: "When in a Fog, Light up Your Wog."

A most outstanding production of *The Monkey's Paw*, by W. W. Jacobs, was put on by Norman Carter, an Aussie, and a selected cast. Colonel

Black played the father, Carter the mother, and Captain Ted Campbell and Lieutenant Peter Rossiter, also Aussies, had supporting roles.

I lectured on the oil industry in Texas and answered questions about politics in the States. There were many lectures, but none of us will forget the one given by Captain Morgan.

One afternoon, I was returning from a work detail, when he stopped me, telling me he was planning a lecture on "Retroactive Inhibitions" that evening. I passed the word around, but because of the vagueness of the subject, was able to interest only fifty men in attending. Unfortunately, he was actively disliked by all nationalities and prisoners who would have listened to almost any lecture stayed in their huts.

We listened attentively during the lecture, but concluded that it was either beyond our comprehension or pure balderdash. After the lecture, an Aussie, Dr. Sailes, who had taught in a university, walked up to Morgan and congratulated him. "Captain Morgan, I have never heard a lecture like that in my life," we heard him say to the beaming lecturer.

It was the following day after our work detail before we had the opportunity to talk to Dr. Sailes and inquire about it. We asked him to explain what the captain had been talking about.

Dr. Sailes had a twinkle in his brown eyes. "Don't let it worry you, my lads, I taught philosophy, not psychology, but I have read widely on the latter. We have had Freud, Addler, and many others, but Captain Morgan is in a class by himself. His school might be called echolalia. Look it up and you'll understand what I mean." He smiled broadly, shook his grey curls back from his ears, and told us to see Dr. Rosenburg, a gynecologist who had a medical dictionary.

When we found the gynecologist and asked him about the word he laughed. We repeated our conversation with the professor and were told that Dr. Sailes was extremely fond of a joke. We soon learned that echolalia was a symptom of a psychiatric condition, meaning the patient was enamored with the sound of his own voice.

Of such foolishness were some of our days composed. Anything to relieve the tedium of prison life was welcome.

About this time the Japanese requested volunteers to tell the people at home what magnificent treatment we were receiving. Radio broadcasts were to be made to America via Australia. Johnny Sayre volunteered. He made a speech about the fine treatment the Japs were dispensing.

"Don't forget to tell our people in the States what really wonderful things the Japanese are doing for us. Tell them how well we are treated. Tell the Army, tell the Navy, but by all means, tell it to the Marines!"

Sargent Katazumi also volunteered and said he wished, most particularly, to send his very best regards to his Uncle Sam. The Japs beamed at what they felt was marvelous cooperation from the prisoners.

After completion of the broadcast, the Bash Artist, who never seemed to get sent anywhere when the other guards were transferred, came over to Chuck, Gordon, and me, and actually smiled: "You are very fortunate. You are moving to a land of milk and honey!" He waited expectantly for some reaction from us.

Since any change interested us intensely, we obliged him by asking innumerable questions about the proposed move. He kept repeating that the only thing he knew about it was that it was a Land of Milk and Honey. The Japs exaggerated to such a degree that we could put no credence in anything they said.

We finally gave up on the Bash Artist and questioned other guards who spoke more English. They told us we were probably going to Burma. This elated us, since we had heard on our hidden radios that the Allied troops were in Burma and we felt we stood a better chance of effecting an escape.

"The Allies might even swoop down and release us," said Mike.

"But let me tell you one thing," an Aussie newspaperman confided, "I've been to Burma, and you can believe me, it is no land of milk and honey."

"Well," replied Tex, "the way I have it figured, we must be going to hell!"

"Whatcha mean?" asked Mike.

"Well," replied Tex, "the way the Japs exaggerate, they'd be sure to describe Hell as a Land of Milk and Honey if they were in charge of it!"

CHAPTER 10

To the Land of Milk and Honey

The month of September came and went and we were still at Batavia. On the evening of October 1, the Bash Artist, followed by several young Korean guards, walked into our barracks and informed us that 175 of the American prisoners were to leave for an unannounced destination the following morning. I was to be part of this group.

I returned to the barracks in a state of high excitement. Gordon was frankly doubtful, but since many of the other men had heard the same thing, we shelved our doubts and pandemonium broke loose. Men who were not going began giving me lists of their relatives in the States, and messages to be delivered to them. This erased any doubt from my mind that we were going.

We rushed about camp collecting our gear, and an odd assortment it was: old wire, pails, sacks, pieces of rope, books, old cooking utensils and extra clothing, such as it was. If we did not go to Burma, most of it could be discarded; if we were not exchanged, it might well prove more valuable than the crown jewels, because we could not replace it.

While packing, the thought of exchange kept my pulses pounding. I dropped things, looked for things I had already packed, and did my share of generally fouling up the detail. There was one thing I did not need to be told: my mind was not on my work but back home in Texas.

I scarcely heard the conversations of my friends, who were occupied in devising elaborate plans to overcome the guards when we reached Burma. Others speculated about the effects of wartime rationing in the States. Rationing or not, they planned luscious, delicious-sounding meals. One food item was conspicuous by its absence from their menus—rice!

I lay down on my sack, hoping sleep would come, but instead, one by one, the faces of my family drifted before me. I could hear my father's hearty laugh; I could see my girl, Alicia, in a blue dress that matched her eyes. The images were too much for me. My morale soared and soared and I felt myself caught up in a cloud of excitement, created by my conviction that this was to be a homecoming to end all of its kind. Sleep was utterly out of the question.

Sometime toward morning the guards came in with a list bearing the names of 16 more men who were going with us. We scrambled madly about dividing the food once more, and before we were back in our bunks, dawn was arriving and reveille was sounding

Breakfast was lavish. Many of us were nauseated from the excitement and could not touch it. We had been broken out at 0500, and told to be ready for *tenko* in an hour. At 0530 a Jap officer stomped in, saw we were not yet ready and flew into a rage. He spoke no English, but rushed about screaming "Speed-o, speed-o!" until I wanted to wring his neck to end the noise.

The Korean guards arrived as usual, giving their orders for us to polish their shoes, carry their gear and sweep the floor. The Jap officer countermanded their orders and the guards bashed us for not following their orders. Our officers tried to calm the general atmosphere by helping us pack, but their sudden appearance threw the guards into a further snit. They, in turn, began striking the American officers. It was beyond the comprehension of all the guards when, for any reason whatever, we departed from the set routine.

Despite the rushing about, it was more than three hours before the orders were given for us to pack ourselves into the trucks and head for the docks. The final count was 191 Yanks, including four American officers, and 250 Australians.

The trip to the docks gave me an opportunity to observe the vast change that had been wrought in the appearance of the city of Batavia. Buildings were shells, statues were decapitated, and only the houses and

U.S.S. *Houston* (CA30).

Aircraft Practice on the
Houston.

Commanding Officer, Captain Albert H
Rooks, U.S.S. *Houston* (CA-30) inspecting his
ship's crew, circa 1940-1941. Courtesy of Otto
Schwartz, U.S.S. *Houston* Association, 1982.
U.S. Naval History and Heritage Command
Photograph.

President Franklin D. Roosevelt waving from the deck of the U.S.S. *Houston*.

James Gee in his dress blues, pre-war.

Summer, 1941: photo of the U.S.S. *Houston* (CA–30)'s Marine Detachment. James Gee is in the back row, 5th Marine from the left. By the time the *Houston* went into her last battle (1 March 1942), the detachment had swelled in size to 74 Marines. Only 34 survived the last battle at Sunda Strait. All were captured on Java by Imperial Japanese forces. By the time the Pacific War ended, only 29 Marines had survived the POW camps of the Japanese.

Death Railway view from the train, showing the challenging terrain over which the POWs had to build the railway.

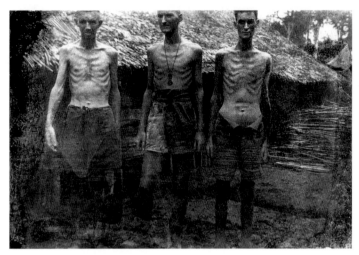

1943 Thai–Burma Railway POWs.

Hellfire railway pass.

POWs early on in their internment.

Australian and British prisoners of war lay track on the Burma–Thailand railway, 1943.

U.S.S. *Houston's* colors at half-mast after returning from the funeral party— note damage of the mainmast, Tjilatjap.

61. Entering Tjilatjap, Java, N.E.I.,
MARBLEHEAD passed close aboard HOUSTON,
which had already made port following the
same action. Damage abaft her mainmast
was quite apparent. HOUSTON's colors are
half-masted pending return of her funeral
party.

FLOWERS IN THE CHURCH

The flowers were placed in the Church today by the Young People of the Church, honoring the memory of James Wallace Gee. "Jimmy," who went down on the Cruiser Houston in the battle of Java, was a former leader of our young people while a student at the University of Texas.

Information on the back of the church program describing the memorial service his parents had held for James Gee when it was mistakenly thought he had not survived the sinking of his ship.

Kanchanaburi Cemetery where there is a memorial monument thanking the Allies for their service.

James Gee's Lost Battalion grave medallion.

Jimmy Gee at the time of the liberation of his
POW camp, 1945.

The telegram sent from U.S. Fleet Hospital, Guam, notifying Jimmy's parents that he was alive.
October 3, 1945.

James Gee's release date.

The staff of the Guantanamo Bay medical facility. On the left is Rosalie in her wheelchair, recovering from malaria contracted while serving as Charge Nurse of the Psychiatric Unit.

factories needed by the enemy still contained furnishings and machinery. The place was scarcely recognizable.

While I gawked at the devastation, Chuck suddenly jammed an elbow into my ribs. Since they had less padding than formerly, this was not something I appreciated.

"Take it easy," I said irritably. "What are you doing—subbing for Bash Artist?"

"Look in the cab of the truck when it turns the corner." He pointed toward another truck ahead of us. I watched the truck as it went into the turn, and saw our least favorite officer, Captain Morgan, riding in the cab with the Jap driver.

"Morgan and his shadow," I commented sadly.

"Too bad we couldn't leave an old buddy or two behind," Marv Miller sighed.

We were all quiet for a few seconds, then Johnny Sayre broke into a song with "Me and My Shadow," and the rest of us took it up.

We arrived at the docks and were unloaded. Our old Jap guard, Nasaki, stood looking at an ancient cargo ship in the harbor and shaking his head. "No exchange!" he said. "You go Burma. Ship *dommi-dommi*, *food dommi-dommi, Japan dommi-dommi." Dommi-dommi* meant bad. This, we didn't especially want to hear.

John and I had been sitting on the edge of the dock waiting for the Japs to give the order to embark. After the rush to get us to the docks, the ship was not ready. We had been sitting for almost an hour watching an old guard make coffee for the Japs. After a sleepless night and no breakfast, we were growing faint. Both of us had been trying to think of a way to wangle a cup of coffee from the old man, when suddenly he beckoned to us.

At first, we hadn't recognized Nasaki from the Serang camp. His clothing was tattered, his toes coming through his rubber-soled canvas shoes and he looked wan and gaunt and very old.

He gave us cup after cup of strong coffee, insisting that we use a great deal of sugar in it. While we drank gratefully, he poured forth his troubles. He said he was sick to death of the war, half-starved and worried about his wife and four children in the homeland. He told us he had had nothing but hard work and privation since he had seen us last. As he talked, huge tears rolled down his cheeks, poured over the end of his nose, splashing onto the rough boards of the dock.

I felt a strong surge of pity for the old guard and wished that I could alleviate his troubles. Why, I wondered, when war created tragedy, carnage and displacement, had man not found a better solution to his problems? It was barbarism, because a war settled nothing. Even the victorious party lost huge sums of money; millions of men and often women and children lost their lives in a war the size of this one. And, the time lost in a destructive enterprise such as war—would that, too, not run into billions, if men were paid by the hour? What an aggravating business it was.

Nasaki interrupted my thoughts by shoving two bags of the priceless coffee into my hands.

"Hope friends have better life soon," he said, his eyes full of misery. "Japan no win war!"

I thanked him for the coffee and for the kind wishes. He had called us his friends.

As we walked back to the end of the dock, I kept thinking he represented the best of the Japanese, apart from all the militarism. I had to admit that his conduct was a far cry from the behavior of most of the guards.

What lay ahead? I didn't wish to think about it. Perhaps I had known all along that we were not to be exchanged. What would The Land of Milk and Honey be like? I tried not to visualize it. I had read Kipling. I knew the song "On the Road to Mandalay," but whether or not the sun came up like thunder—I could not, at this point, care less. I was not going home. That was a single, sad, solitary fact. I knew precious little about Burma and did not feel anxious to learn more. But, then, we had not actually been given a choice.

★

It was early afternoon when we were loaded onto the incinerator-like old Japanese tub, which had no portholes, and which was, as Mike put it, "Hotter'n twenty acres of burnin' stumps!" No one had room to stretch out and there was barely room to sit upright. Our quarters were located on a half deck which had been built between the main and second decks. It was impossible to keep from colliding with your neighbor.

We were on the old tub for three days and three nights and, inevitably, many men came down with dysentery. It was difficult to make the ascent by way of a rickety ladder from the hold to the main deck under the best of circumstances. The latrines were topside. Some of the ill men found negotiating the ladder too difficult, even with help, and the resulting stench in the hold was overpowering.

Sleep was quite impossible, except in snatches. There was not room enough to lie down and the roll of the ship kept throwing us against each other. Added to the heat, lack of room, stench of crap and vomit, was another problem—rats running over our bodies when we attempted to doze. We finally arrived in Singapore harbor where we spent the most miserable night of the trip. The old cargo ship was hot enough while underway, but standing still she was an oven. Perspiration poured off of us and we suffered miserably from thirst, particularly the men with dysentery who were extremely dehydrated to begin with.

The next morning we were removed from the ship and loaded onto trucks. My muscles were so stiff that they felt that they belonged to someone else. Only one who had shared this nightmare voyage could appreciate the relief we felt at being able to once again stand on terra firma and to feel the cool, fresh breeze on our faces.

We were driven along flat land with tropical vegetation. Palm trees waved gently in the trade wind, there was blue sky above and, here and there, a patch of cumulus clouds competed with the blue of the surrounding ocean. All looked peaceful, if you could just exclude the Jap guards.

We arrived at a sort of green meadow, surrounded by a high stone wall. At the northern end of the wall was a weather-beaten, almost windowless building, with sentry boxes occupied by sour-looking Jap sentries who could overlook the surrounding countryside from their perches.

Despite the hot Malay sunshine, the sight of the prison sent a chill down my spine. All of us had heard the horror stories about enemy prisons. Rohan Rivitt, an Aussie journalist, had been a prisoner in a

Serang jail and many others among us had had some experiences along this line.

We had excellent reasons for being apprehensive about Changi Prison. Our feelings of apprehension were not justified, however, at least not this time. Once unloaded, as though having second thoughts, the Japs ordered us back onto the trucks and we were driven a short distance to a camp administered by the British. Tall Sikh guards, their brown skin glistening in the bright sunshine patrolled the high stone walls surrounding the large camp.

We were exhausted and wanted nothing so much as a chance to stretch out and get some overdue sleep. The British officers had other plans for us. We were served a wretched meal of worse-than-average prison-camp rice filled with small stones and a practically inedible stew. They then set us to digging latrines, mowing grass, pushing heavy carts and chopping wood. The British enlisted men lolled in their barracks.

Many of our working men were ill, but in addition to the heavy tasks assigned to us, the British officers, wearing short trousers and carrying canes, paraded like peacocks before our bedraggled crew, demanding that we salute them.

On the following morning, when we were again assigned work details, while the British enlisted men goldbricked, we complained to Captain Morgan. He showed little sympathy. He ate with the British officers and did no work; therefore, he apparently saw nothing amiss in the general setup.

Nothing happened. We waited. On the third day, while Bob and Chuck were cutting wood, they had occasion to see the food eaten by the British enlisted men. They reported to us that the British prisoners ate better food than ours, cooked by wood which we cut, and not only had American Red Cross food with every meal, but between meals, too. We blew our collective tops!

We called on Captain Morgan. I was too angry to talk, but my voice was not needed. Chuck and Marv gave him a detailed account of exactly how we felt. We were gathered in a circle around Morgan and for the first time he appeared to be somewhat frightened. He promised, with seriousness in his tone, that he would look into the situation.

Immediately after this talk, I went with Chuck and Marv to our woodcutting detail. We worked all morning in the hot sun, perspiration streaming down our backs because of the beastly humidity. We were ravenously hungry. The hard physical labor on scant rations was too much.

Our morning's work finished and our knees almost buckling from exhaustion, we wondered whether or not we could make it back to camp. Looking about for something to sustain us, our eyes scanned a clump of coconut trees loaded with fruit. We looked at each other and nodded, then, taking our axes, we quickly worked off some of our hostility toward the British by cutting down four of the trees.

We had scarcely struck the last blow when two irate sergeants from His Majesty's Army swooped down on us, yelling at the top of their voices. "Why, you G … D … Yanks! Stop it! Stop it! How dare you use your bloody axes for cutting down the King's coconut trees? I say, stop it! Stop it!"

Not having had a chance to eat or drink from our prizes, we were not about to be frustrated by having them snatched from us. Stretching himself to his full height above the shorter of the sergeants, Chuck glowered menacingly at him. The sergeant took a step toward the coconuts. Chuck swung his axe over his right shoulder as though he intended using it.

"It's not bloody yet," he told the sergeant in a tone that was deceptively calm, "and bloody don't mean quite the same to an American than it does to you. Take one more step toward those coconuts and I'll cut your G … D … head off—and you'll see what bloody means in our country."

The astounded sergeant stepped backward. "But those are the King's coconuts!"

Chuck doubled up his huge right fist, slamming it into his left palm three times in rapid succession. The tattoo of an eagle on the back of his right hand stood out clearly in the bright sunshine—an indigo blue etching.

"Right now, you food-stealing bastard, hunger is king, so get lost!" he bellowed.

The sergeant retreated to a pair of trees at the back of the clearing. While they watched us with puzzled expressions, we enjoyed several of the coconuts, throwing the remainder into the wood carts to take back to our friends in camp.

We had gone only a short distance when the sergeants overtook us. The short one gave Chuck a big smile. "I say, old boy," he said, "you wouldn't really have cut me blinkin' 'ead off, now would ya?"

Chuck's face took on a stern expression and without a word, he reached into the wood cart and, picking up his axe, swung it viciously above the short sergeant's head. The Brit blanched, gulped and started to run, the second sergeant following close at his heels.

Chuck took another swing at their retreating backs and boomed after them, "If we don't get some food, we're gonna eat you!" He lowered his voice and, putting the axe back into the cart, said musingly, "You know, my dad always said that hungry people are the meanest dang critters in the world."

CHAPTER 11

Moulmein Jail

Toward the end of October we were jammed into an even dirtier, hotter cargo ship for the trip to Burma. Chuck Satterlee was fortunate in finding a perch atop a large tractor, which kept him high above sweating bodies—but not for long. The rest of us were relegated to the bottom of the hold along with an assortment of machinery and Captain Morgan ordered Chuck down with the rest of us.

"It's useless to be resentful, Satterlee," he told the fuming Chuck. "You know one officer is worth ten enlisted men."

"The day will come, you son of a bitch," Chuck shot at him, "when the whole world won't gyrate around your cotton-pickin' ass!"

We were brought topside for chow but most of us returned to the hold without eating. The food was nauseating and inedible.

We finally fell asleep draped over the machinery and each other. The roar of planes brought us awake in terror. We waited, praying not to be blown to bits, while the planes crossed and recrossed over the ship. We knew the Jap soldiers and guards would be the first to leave the ship in any scramble for safety. The one tiny hatch for hundreds of men was inadequate to say the least. Then there were the sick. A number had been left at Changi, but others had not been considered sick enough to be left behind. They were, however, weak and gaunt from dysentery; the heat and lack of sufficient food and water was not improving their condition. If we found it necessary to abandon ship, they would be too debilitated to swim more than a few strokes.

The roar of planes overhead began to fade, yet sleep refused to come after this incident. The foul air and the heat prevented sleep and the thought that the next few minutes might be our last did not help. We took turns fanning the air over the sick.

We arrived, finally, in Rangoon harbor and, while we were being loaded onto a larger, gravel-bearing ship, we had a pleasant surprise. Allied bombers had been active here. Small boats littered the Irrawaddy River, their keels splintered, masts broken and huge gaping holes in the larger disabled ones. Everywhere we looked, wrecks littered the main channel. Neither docks nor buildings had been spared and all about the town of Rangoon was vivid evidence that this was not, after all, a one-sided war.

The disastrous appearance of the town seemed to have a sobering effect upon our merry guards. Their behavior toward the sick on the voyage could only be described as outrageous, but having observed the chaos that had once been the capital of Burma, they appeared to be thoughtful—gave us time to help the ill without jabbing them with guns—and allowed all of us to stretch out on the gravel.

We scarcely felt the rough gravel—to stretch out was a tremendous luxury. Darkness fell as we started up the Irrawaddy and the guards allowed us to move the sick out onto the decks for fresh air. An enormous orange moon hung over us and the heavy fragrance of the tropics floated across the deck. The screams of wild animals mingled with the moans of the sick and the constant cursing of the guards. I had seen semi-jungle before, but nothing like this outside of a Tarzan movie.

By dusk of the following day, we arrived at the mouth of the Salween River, where we were transferred onto a huge barge pulled by tugs. Close to midnight we arrived at Moulmein, where we were unloaded and marched to the Moulmein jail.

The Moulmein jail was something you might see in a nightmare and feel immensely relieved when you awoke. I never expected to spend any time in jail and to be incarcerated in this pest house was enough to send all of us to the loony bin. We had had almost no mental illness before coming to Burma, but the combination of the ordeal on the cargo ship and the Moulmein jail soon had another of our men hearing the voices of their friends at home, and their families in the chimes of the pagoda.

The jail was surrounded by a high stone wall. On the hills above it were the houses of Moulmein and on the top of the highest hill stood the large gold-tipped pagoda made famous by Kipling. Each time a breeze swept through its bells sent out their chimes. In a wooden barracks native criminals and POWs were housed and in its center, lepers were kept. Punishment was meted out with a giant-sized bullwhip.

On our first night we slept on the hard floor of the jail. Our pillows were wooden blocks, effectively cutting off any circulation to the brain which might have interfered with our sleep. Despite the less-than-ideal conditions, we slept. We could stretch our legs, something we had been unable to do for almost three weeks on the hell ships.

When morning came, the sun, true to Kipling's description, did come up like thunder. We could see the red-tiled homes above the jail, some of them very attractive, surrounded by waving palms and climbing flowers in full bloom. Whether the gold pagoda was the one written about was not one of our most pressing considerations at this point.

Tex, Mike, Gordon, and John joined me in a tour of the jail. Tex expressed concern that we would be unable to trade with the natives because of the high stone wall.

"It just don't matter anymore!" Mike complained, shaking his long, shaggy, yellow hair in mock despair. "I've near give up tryin' to stay up anyway. My pa always said, 'Now be sure and stay out of jail, son.' How can a feller stay out of jail? I'd be in jail for stealin' food if I could find any. I might even get taken for murder for eatin' one of them little squinty-eyed guards, but anybody with half an eye could see they're all gristle and they wouldn't be worth dullin' your knife skinnin' them!"

"Jail is bad enough," Tex replied, "but I get a genuine skeerdy feelin' lookin' at that bullwhip."

Breakfast did nothing to raise our spirits. The menu sported two choices in minute quantities and we took both—rice and sweet potato leaves.

After breakfast we had a serious discussion about our food supply and the prospects for replenishing our stocks. We still had a few tins which were being carefully guarded for a real emergency.

After assessing the direness of the situation, we concluded that, unless we supplemented the food of the ill POWs, they would surely die. These cans were some of the issue for our Christmas dinner and some of them had already been opened for the dysentery patients while we were on the hell ships. It was quite obvious they would never see another Christmas unless we made a constructive effort to feed them.

I sat down on the jail floor with Tex, Mike, Gordon, John, Bob and Chuck and placed the canned goods in a circle.

"Since this seems to be all there is between me and starvation, I would like to just look at it a while before I play the Good Samaritan and give it away," John sighed, sadly.

"Do you want to change your mind, guy?" Marv inquired.

We had all voted to give the food away, but it was not difficult to understand that some of the POWs might feel they were setting their own death sentences. In our emaciated condition it was quite obvious that none of us could last long unless our food improved remarkably or we were allowed to improve the menu by trading with the natives.

Gordon stared pensively at our meager horde. "It looks bad," he said, at last, "but you know it's the people who give things away that never seem to need them. I couldn't eat this food knowing those guys were dying 'cause I ate it."

"I admire your faith," Bob murmured, "but when the guards won't even let us talk to the native criminals where to do think we'll get more food? Doesn't it seem a bit unlikely?"

"That's not our problem. Somebody upstairs will take care of it. We haven't died in eight months. I believe in miracles. I don't say a big steak may walk into this jail, but we'll get some food."

"We all know miracles used to happen in past times, but just name me one that's happened in the last century and I'll put in with you. Now don't, please, give me that every hair in your head is counted routine, or God-takes-care-of-the-sparrow-stuff. He didn't ask anyone to be stupid. Where will the food come from?" This speech was from Marv Miller.

"Yeah," Bob chimed in. "We all know about the water into wine—the loaves and fishes—the storms that subsided—the lepers that were cleansed—the dead that were raised to life." He paused, "But name a modern miracle."

I suddenly remembered something and told them how the grasshoppers had been eating the Mormons' crops and they had prayed for the Lord to save their crops. Seagulls had appeared, hundreds of miles from the sea, and had eaten the grasshoppers. I was not a Mormon, but that had happened about 1847, shortly after the Mormons had entered the valley in Utah.

Bob sat in his usual thoughtful pose, his stubby right forefinger on the end of his nose, his thumb beneath his chin. Whenever he was in deep thought he propped his right elbow on his right knee and assumed this familiar pose. "That," he conceded, "couldn't be anything *but* a miracle! What would seagulls be doing in Utah, for Heaven's sakes! Hmmm."

"Shhhhh!" whispered Tex, rather frantically, I thought. Slowly, while we all watched curiously, he stealthily turned his long frame about and began to creep on his hands and knees toward the wooden block where he slept. We sat like six wooden Indians while he slipped a warm uniform coat from his role of personal possessions. I had no idea what he intended doing with it, but in watching his handsome, brown face, taut with a strange intensity, it occurred to me that he looked precisely as a wild animal might look before springing upon its prey. What prey, I wondered? Then, I saw it! Lying along the studs of the wooden jail was a fat, glistening, brown snake, its eyes closed in apparent sleep.

"Fresh meat!" gurgled Mike, excitedly. No one else said a word as he, too, began to crawl on his hands and knees, but in a different direction. He made it to the door of the barracks without awakening the prize and carefully broke a small switch from a bush growing there.

The drama ended in less time than it takes to recount it. Tex sprang with the coat, throwing it over the unsuspecting reptile. When coat, snake and Mike landed on the floor near us, Mike was ready with his switch and, as the snake darted out of the coat, he struck countless rapid blows across its spine, paralyzing it. Chuck finished it off by crushing its head with a heavy tin of corned beef.

"Miracle or not, we have meat for supper," said Tex. "But first, I reckon I'd better ask that Burmese warden if it's poison or not."

He started to reach for the snake, but suddenly the bloody reptile, lying on the wooden floor, began to twitch its tail furiously. All of us jumped to our feet, except Tex, who was bending over it in an imperturbable fashion.

"That snake is still alive, lame brains!" yelled Chuck.

I felt somewhat apprehensive. I had had never seen a reptile like this one and the ferocity with which it was flailing its tail about was disconcerting in the small space.

Tex looked at us in disbelief and disgust, his heavy, black brows drawn together. "How are you young 'uns doin' in Kindergarten?" he asked, his tone more one of pity than censure. He lifted the snake by the back of its head and shook it. It was fat, large and although snake had never been a favorite entrée of mine, this being the first time, I could see the possibilities.

"Simmer down!" Tex advised, then added, ruefully: "I reckon I knew you fellers didn't know too much about varmints and snakes and things, but I figgered every damn fool in the whole world learned at his mammy's knee that a snake wiggles its tail till sundown—no matter if it's deader than a doornail, which this one *is*!" He strode off in the direction of the warden's office.

Tex was lean and dark and fierce. There was something of a wild animal look about him. His movements were quick and sure and, in spite of his great height, he navigated like a jungle cat.

"That guy walks like an Indian," Bob said as he turned to Mike. "Are you sure he doesn't have some Indian blood, Mike?"

"Mule, maybe, but no Indian. We don't have no furriners where we come from."

The rest of us spent several frustrating minutes trying to explain to Mike that the American Indians were natives—until we began to realize that he was kidding us.

"We don't have any Indians, though. I've seen Mexicans, but we don't have any of those in our neighborhood. I like their cooking, but we don't have them. We have two kinds of people. We have white trash and people who work for a living.

"The people who own the farms take care of people who get in trouble. Nobody can starve to death in Texas unless he has both hands tied behind him and I s'pose some good-hearted woman would still stop by and feed him with a spoon. Chicken broth—that stuff—maybe custard. Where'd Tex go with that snake? I'm starved!"

We gathered our tinned goods and started to distribute them to the section of the jail where 15 of our men were desperately ill.

Near the end of the first week in Moulmein jail, Chuck came rushing into our barracks in an agitated state. We had been discussing our plight. Morale was at a low ebb and malnutrition was beginning to affect our thinking processes. The intense heat, the lack of any mental stimulation, the frenzy over our scant food supply and the atmosphere of the jail seemed to be pushing us over the brink into mental derangement.

We followed Chuck outside. What I saw made me rub my eyes in disbelief and do a double take. It was incredible that these men—new arrivals—most of whom who had left Batavia in reasonably good condition only three weeks before, were now literally walking skeletons. I asked Vandermast, a Dutchman we had known at the Bicycle Camp, what had happened to them.

They were without exception hollow-eyed, their skin chalk white and sagging over bones from which most of the supporting flesh had totally disappeared. Only their bellies were fat, bloated from malnutrition.

"Let me sit down before I fall down," Vandermast said weakly.

I brought him a tin cup of boiled water and he sat down upon his gear. We listened in horror while he recounted the almost unbelievable story of their nightmare voyage from Batavia to Burma.

"The Japs took twenty-two days to get us to Rangoon, he began, stopping between words to catch his breath. "We were attacked by an Allied submarine and the Japs kept us nine days in Penang harbor without letting us out of the hell ship. A lot of us were already sick with dysentery. An epidemic hit us and by the time we were moved from that hell ship's hold, we had fourteen corpses to keep us company."

I suggested he lie down for a few minutes before he attempted to tell us the rest of the story. He shook his head emphatically.

"I've got to tell it, Jim," he said. "I might not live very long and you and these fellows must make sure the tale gets back, to let people know what murdering bastards these Japs really are."

Vandermast resumed after a while: "A Jap doctor was sent to decide what to do with us. He sent us to Rangoon jail where we were locked in a cell with nothing but straw on the floor. We had no bedding, no utensils and no medicine. In a few days there were two hundred and sixty of us dead—and four hundred more dead than alive. The Japs gave us nothing except tools to bury the corpses.

"They finally took the strongest of us and sent us to the hospital. It was almost as bad as the jail. The only reason I was picked to go was because they knew I spoke Japanese and they needed interpreters. The Jap doctor told me that four days from now all of us who can walk will be sent into the jungle to build a railroad. He said I would have to go because interpreters were needed up the line. Do you think I'll make it?" he asked Riley.

"As long as we have life, there is hope, Van," I said. "None of us is in perfect physical condition, but if we get outside of these walls in three days, we'll find food somewhere, you can be sure."

The arrival of noon chow prevented our discussing it further until we had eaten. I was grateful for this. It was obvious from his present condition that he needed months in a hospital and the best of medical attention to fully recover.

Noon chow always consisted of pie melon, which we called "White Death" and which tasted precisely like a gourd.

Three days later we were ready for our march across town. We were filled with misgivings about appearing in the sight of the natives. The jeers and insults of the Japanese still rang in our ears. We could only expect the same from the Burmese. We couldn't have been more wrong. As the railroad cars into which we had been loaded for the trip into the jungle passed through Moulmein, the Burmese men, women and children lined the streets, many of them openly weeping. They tore food from their stalls and threw it to us. Cheroots, tobacco, fruit and rice cakes. Women rushed from their huts with trays of native biscuits, freshly baked for the day, and, risking the wrath of the guards, dumped them into our hands.

Many of them wore filthy clothing and the stench from some huts was overpowering, but we gratefully took and ravenously ate the foodstuffs. They looked for all the world like a host of angels. They had shown us a loyalty which was like a Christmas present after the long months of native hostility. They were obviously loyal to the British.

Sometimes a man or a woman moved close to the cars to yell words of encouragement to us. "The Yanks are coming!" or "White man come soon!" or "Not long now!" These words were a tonic to our weary spirits. We had been mistreated for such a long time that we had all but forgotten that there were people on our side.

The trip to the main rail center, Thanbyuzat, from where all POWs were dispatched to the railroad jungle camps, was made by a small rail car, pulled by a tiny, wood-burning engine. We passed through rich agricultural lands where Burmese were plowing with water buffalo and working their crops. At least there was food in Burma—if we could only get our hands on it. Just the sight of its availability cheered us immensely. We also passed banana trees and rubber plantations.

Thanbyuzat was a supply and rail center made up of dark and dilapidated bamboo huts with roofs of attap. Some of these were euphemistically referred to by the Japs as the "Main Hospital" where row upon row of patients lay on bare bamboo slats or platforms.

It was late afternoon when we arrived and stored our gear in the hut provided. Almost at once we saw Earl Scott, an Aussie we had known in Java. He was hospitalized with dysentery and malaria. He told us that the jungle camps were rated from bad to impossible. They were designated according to the number of kilometers in distance from Thanbyuzat.

We were to go to 40 Kilo Camp, the most remote at present, to help build a railroad through jungle never before penetrated by man. The Japs were trying to build a railroad to connect the Moulmein–Ye line with the main Singapore–Bangkok line, running south into Siam, or Thailand, and along the peninsula. There were only three activated camps at present.

"There are about three thousand Aussies under Brigadier Varley, or mostly Aussies," Scott told me. "He's in charge of our branch which is called Number Three Thai Prisoners of War. There are about five thousand Dutch and also two thousand Americans, Aussies and Brits arriving sometime after Christmas, the grapevine says. The two thousand are Number Five Branch POWs. The Dutch are mostly from Sumatra and Java. What a hell of a way to fight a war!"

The hospital had no floor. Bamboo beds were three feet from the soil. Several hundred patients occupied the beds.

CHAPTER 12

Workin' on the Railroad

While we were mulling over the problems involved in forcing our group of skinny POWs to build a railroad through impenetrable jungle, with workers on the verge of collapse from starvation, the guards interrupted us to tell us about our duties.

I was assigned to the *buppin* or wood-cutting crew, as were Tex, Marv, Chuck and others. Our bad luck held out when we were assigned Captain Morgan as our *kumicho*, our boss.

Even Gordon complained. "I must admit," said he, "that that guy is harder to shake than the seven-year itch and twice as aggravating!"

"Never mind about that," Chuck put in dourly, "that old boy's had his last assignment. He'll just have to end up in the jungle with a tree wrapped around his neck." A light shown in his eyes as though he were anticipating Christmas presents. "Shit!" he said, suddenly, rubbing his hands together. His sudden enthusiasm was alarming. None of us felt that Chuck would commit murder, but I could scarcely suppress a feeling of uneasiness. It was not a pleasant situation to watch one member of our group grow fat, have plenty of cigarettes, and good clothing, while the rest of us went without.

Most of the prisoners were forced to walk the distance to the camp. We were fortunate to be on the *buppin* crew and were driven to the campsite in trucks in order to get it ready for the others. We dug pit latrines, cleared the ground, cut wood for the cook shack and carried water from a creek a mile away.

The camp consisted of a cluster of attap, or palm frond-thatched huts constructed by the natives. A wire fence enclosed the huts and dense jungle surrounded the fence. We could hear strange and eerie sounds coming from the jungle that grew louder as wild animals started their nightly prowl.

As darkness settled over the camp, the Japs ordered us to build a large fire to keep the animals away. Horseface, one of our least-liked guards, stood guard to make sure none of us tried to escape. It was unlikely that any of us had the strength to try after the long day of strenuous labor. I fell asleep at once, only to be awakened by the wild, shrill screams of the jungle animals. This happened repeatedly. Finally, the Bash Artist appeared with wooden clappers to signal the morning.

After *tenko* and chow, the Japanese issued the equipment for working on the railroad. This produced the first really good laugh we had had in some time. In fact, we laughed out loud when the Bash Artist doled out small hoes made of corrugated iron with wooden handles and minute baskets suspending from yo-yo poles.

"If you guys build a railroad with *that* equipment," Bob McCann said doubtfully, "I'll believe it's one of those miracles you're always talking about."

Gordon looked at the tools carefully and commented, "It looks like a long hot summer, but full speed ahead!"

There was no doubt that we were the strangest crew ever collected for doing this type of work. Even the Chinese coolies who had built the Santa Fe had worn more clothing than we sported. We trudged off toward the worksite, clad in G-strings, barefoot and carrying our odd-looking implements. We were accompanied by a few Jap privates wearing faded, patched tan shorts and Japanese Army baseball caps, perched atop towels wound carefully about their heads. I longed for a camera to capture this little tableau, but my amusement was curtailed by Captain Morgan, our great morale builder.

"Hey, you cotton-pickin' rebels!" he yelled. "Get hot before I tell Horseface you're goldbricking!" He sat on a stump, a cigarette dangling from his lips. He was growing quite pudgy from his unknown food supply.

Chuck hooked both huge thumbs beneath his G-string and swaggered toward our *kumicho*. I feared he was asking for trouble, but he was closer to Morgan than he was to me and I could hardly dash up and forcibly restrain him.

"I hear you used to be in the numbers racket in New Jersey," said Chuck. His voice was quite calm and I relaxed somewhat, at the same time wondering how the captain would react to this comment.

I was unprepared for the broad smile that swept Morgan's face. "It's only the stupid guys who work for a living," he said, smugly, shifting a near-full pack of cigarettes in his shirt pocket. I had a strong urge to knock him down and take the pack for the men in the hospital hut. I did not smoke, but I knew a cigarette would dull, if not kill their hunger.

"Yeah, I was in the Big Time in New York," our fearless leader continued, boastfully.

"How come you left?" I queried.

Morgan smiled ruefully and went on: "Things got a little hot. The boss caught me in bed with his doll. He went for his gun and I went out the window. Second story, too! God, but I was shook up!" He stopped to wipe the perspiration from his forehead and, even in retrospect, he looked frightened thinking about his narrow escape. "I coulda been killed!"

"You mean from a two-story fall?" Marv asked.

"Hell, no! The boss left his gun in the other room, or I'd 'a never made it! *That* was a close shave! I coulda been *killed*! I coulda been *shot*!" He rubbed his mustache nervously with a forefinger, his eyes clouding with preoccupation.

"And *that*," drawled Tex, meaningfully, "would have been a durned shame."

There was something in the tone of the towering Tex that made Morgan and the rest of us look at him oddly. It was impossible to tell whether he was being insulting, humorous, or sympathetic. But knowing Tex, I doubted that he was being sympathetic.

"Back to the salt mines," I suggested quickly. "The cooks will be short of wood if we don't hit the detail."

"Yeah," Morgan agreed. "Shove off, you guys. No guard is needed for the *buppin* crew."

We fought our way through vines, bushes and the dense foliage of the jungle toward a cluster of trees. When we were out of sight of

Morgan, we hustled about collecting mangoes, pomelos and tiny crisp green bamboo shoots. Wood-cutting had its brighter side. We sat down and ate gratefully, being careful not to overeat. We had learned from experience that overeating after starvation rations could give stomach cramps worse than hunger.

In mid-afternoon, we started back toward camp with a supply of wood. We intended splitting it and stacking it near the cook shack. Suddenly, Marv put his load on the ground and motioned to Chuck. They held a whispered confab from which we were excluded.

"You guys go ahead," suggested Marv, "and we'll see you in a few minutes." He waved a hand airily, disappearing behind a huge bush. Chuck followed him.

We continued toward camp, arriving just in time to see an enormous bull elephant charging through the Nip shack, scattering guards in every direction. The air was blue with Nipponese expletives, screams and curses.

The guards returned to the scene of the disaster and ordered the POWs to rebuild the shack. The two pranksters sauntered unnoticed by the guards toward the cook shack to deposit their burden of wood. Marv's poker face gave no indication that he had been involved in the charge of the bull, but Chuck burst out laughing as soon as the Nips' backs were turned. Later, both admitted they had been responsible.

While I knew we would be the ones to rebuild the wrecked Jap shack, I could not refrain from a feeling of satisfaction that Marv and Chuck felt up to performing a prank. There had been little to joke about in past months and it was good to find that they had the spirit.

On the second day, after work, we requested permission from the guards to swim in the river near camp. They agreed. I was floating on my back, watching a giant hornbill making weird hissing noises through the holes in its enormous wings, the others splashing around in a small pool. All seemed peaceful when suddenly we were disturbed by a crashing noise. Raising my head, I saw an enormous bull elephant standing on the bank, observing the swimmers with considerable interest. Tired of being a spectator, he decided to join us and began to lumber into the pool. The shrieking POWs scrambled for the bank. Undismayed, the bull wallowed delightedly in the water, which had now become extremely muddy from the thrashing about of his enormous feet. He looked up at us peering from the shore and, filling his trunk with the muddy ooze, proceeded to spray us from head to foot. So much for our swim. We found another spot, much less adapted to our purposes and washed the grime from our bodies and hair.

By the end of a week, since all of us wore G-strings as a total outfit, I had freckles over my entire body, including my backside. Marv delighted in announcing my appearance anywhere with: "Ah, here comes Gee in his G-string!"

Gordon worked on the railroad and regaled us with tales of his trials with his Japanese coworkers, the Imperial Army's privates, whose main assignment seemed to be to keep the POWs producing. "They work like crazy for twenty minutes, then sit down for an hour," he told our *buppin* crew. "They sing all the time and it sounds like they are saying, 'Itch me! Itch me!' It's far worse than static on an old radio! Sometimes I'm tempted to hit them on their beanies with my shovel. If we sing or slow down they bash us. The engineers yell at us, but they never bash us."

The first week was too good to last. The engineers had been educated in the States and they not only saw that we got larger rations per man, but tried to give us some variety. In addition to the rice, we had sweet potatoes, carrots, onions and beef brought by the natives. There was also some dried boxed meat that defied identification. The soldiers and most of the guards showed little serious inclination to bash us, but, after the first week, the Korean guards arrived and the old brutality was again instituted. Within a few days, all of us had a rash of bruises and cuts.

Johnny Sayre, who, for some reason known only to the Japs, was detained in Thanbyuzat, arrived at the end of the second week and was assigned to the cook shack. He told us that the boxed meat was frequently infested with maggots. It was unthinkable to waste food, since no one ever had enough, so the cooks simply cooked the maggots first, by dipping the meat into boiling water until they were dead and then threw the meat in with the vegetables.

The increase in ration gave our morale a lift and changed our entire outlook toward survival. Before, we had wanted to live, but despite our faith, each of us wondered how this could be possible under the existing conditions. Now, our attitude had become that we would live *in spite of* the Japs. There was another factor involved in our uplifted morale. Two radios had been smuggled into camp, piece by piece. While most of us stood guard, a few listened to information on Allied troop movements. It seemed a certainty that the Big Push was not far off. We lay awake at night now, not from hunger or fear, but plotting ways of overcoming the guards.

Outwardly, the Japs remained cruel and our conditions were not improved, except for the food. Gaunt POWs were forced to stand for hours in the scorching sun without food or water, for a trivial or imagined offense. We all bore marks of our captors' brutality. We were cut, bruised, kicked and bashed. We were bloodied, but our heads were unbowed. We felt we could stand anything. Wasn't the Big Push on its way?

Had we known more about the weather, we would have been more alarmed. We learned the hard way. Toward the close of November the monsoon struck. Cold, bone-piercing winds, straight from Siberia, turned our huts into deep freezes. We had neither clothing nor bedding to keep us warm. A few of us still possessed a pair of ragged shorts, but most of us were left with only G-strings.

We built a fire at the end of our hut and sat about, feet tucked beneath us, fists jammed between our knees, arms tight against bony ribcages and teeth chattering. In less time than it takes for me to relate, dozens of men were ill from pneumonia, cat fever and other acute respiratory diseases.

Occasionally, during these nights, we found it necessary to jump up and stomp around in order to restore our circulation. Sleep was out of the question, at least much of the time; so we talked.

I had been extremely fortunate, however, even during the monsoon season, not to come down with any serious illness. I was beginning to wonder how I had managed to be that fortunate when I was assigned to help build a new guard shack (to replace the old one destroyed by the bull elephant.)

It was the third week in November and we had just finished noon chow, consisting of what we called "Blue Danube Stew." The Japs insisted the cooks make a stew of chunks of white pie melon combined with water and a jungle weed that turned the entire concoction a revolting shade of blue. Suddenly, while working on the Nip shack, I began to feel extremely dizzy. I attributed this to the scorching sun and continued my work. My hands, arms and the back of my neck began to feel as though they were on fire and breathing became difficult. I staggered backward and was caught by Chuck, who was helping to build the shack.

"My God, Jim—you look terrible! What's the matter?"

He assisted me back to the barracks, where I stretched out on my bamboo platform. There seemed to be a heavy weight on my chest.

"Better get Doc Cyclops, Chuck," I managed to say. This was the nickname we used for an Aussie army doctor.

Chuck returned in a few minutes with the doctor. Having no thermometer, he took my pulse, looked down my throat and peered down his nose, then announced that he believed I had several degrees of fever. "You probably have dengue, but I have no medication to give you. A few days in bed should cure you. It's nothing to worry about."

I recall looking at the doctor's retreating back, managing to say "Thank you" before lapsing into unconsciousness.

When I awoke it was another day. The sun was rising and I had no recollection of anything having happened after the doctor's call. My head was splitting and my back ached fiercely. I sat up on my platform, the hut revolving wildly about me, and got to my feet. I managed to make it to the latrine, but once there, I fainted. When I regained consciousness, I was back on my cot and Doc Cyclops was bending over me.

"Well, well, well!" he said, peering down his sharp nose, his brows knit in perplexity. "You *are* a very sick young man!"

I did not feel able to make small talk and he continued to regard me, his lips puckered as though someone had drawn them up with a purse string. "You had better stay in bed except for latrine privileges. You have several things wrong with you. You have heat prostration, dengue fever and malnutrition. You'll be all right in a few days, though."

I managed to thank him and he departed once more.

I stayed in bed for three days, growing steadily worse. Each time I walked to the latrine I fainted and either regained consciousness alone, or was helped back to my bunk by one of the other POWs. There were long periods when I didn't know what was transpiring. At other times I had semi-lucid moments. When I was delirious I thought my girl, Alicia, or my mother sat at my bedside. When I attempted to speak to them, however, Alicia's blond curls and pixie beauty dissolved into the chestnut hair and snub-nose of Bob, or my mother's gray curls and dignified charm, with no warning whatever, became the calm face and quiet assurance of my best friend, Gordon Strong.

On the third day, I had chills that shook my bamboo platform; on the fourth day I found I could not move my legs, and, on the fifth, I lapsed into a coma. What happened after that, I later learned from my friends.

Chuck, Gordon, Marv, Mike, Bob, and Tex took turns caring for me when they were not on work details. They begged Doc Cyclops to visit me, but he steadfastly refused. He told them he had no medicine to give me. On the day I became comatose he told Gordon Strong there was nothing he could do.

I might as well tell you," he announced. "That man is going to die."

"Oh, no, he isn't!" Gordon retorted.

Gordon got the fellows together and said special prayers for my recovery, refusing to accept the doctor's prognosis. When the prayers were finished, they discussed my symptoms, deciding that I must have malaria. They went from prisoner to prisoner, begging quinine until they had enough for one large dose. Someone donated two aspirin tablets, which in the Burmese jungle, were more priceless than gold.

Their most difficult problem was getting me to swallow the pills in my delirious state. They managed, and then piled all the clothing they could borrow on top of me and took turns watching throughout the night. No one but Gordon expected me to live.

When the long night's vigil had ended I was still alive, but that was about as much as could be said for me. My friends were forced to report to their details, but someone always remained behind and watched over me.

A new group of POWs arrived at 40 Kilo Camp. Among them was Dr. Hekking, a Dutch doctor, the most wonderful doctor ever to take the Hippocratic Oath. Having given me a complete physical exam from one end to the other, he pronounced that I had a severe case of malaria, complicated by beriberi. He produced some quinine from no one knew where—because none of the other medics was able to procure it—and gave me a large dose.

The quinine made me extremely nauseated, but the fever started to abate and I began to recover. Dr Hekking was in constant attendance; he was a most dedicated man. He told me, as soon as my muddled head cleared somewhat, that I must have fresh fruits and vegetables if I wished to regain the use of my dead legs.

Once more the faithful crew went to bat for me. I was quite astounded at the food they produced. They not only brought me fruit and fresh vegetables, but eggs, broth and other special foods. I will never know how many beatings they took from the Japs while procuring these things. On many occasions I had done the same things these men were doing, but I had never realized how much it meant to the ill man to be fed, bathed and attended to. My friends and Dr. Hekking saved my life.

The small creek at 40 Kilo dried up and we were transferred to 26 Kilo Camp.

Two weeks after the arrival of Dr. Hekking I was able to be transferred to Thanbyuzat. By the end of three weeks, I could sit up in bed, but it was six full weeks before I regained the use of my legs sufficiently to navigate the distance around my bunk. Even then it was necessary to lean heavily on two canes that Earl Scott had made for me.

The hospital at Thanbyuzat was filled to overflowing with nearly a thousand patients, suffering from burns, dysentery, beriberi, heart disease, pneumonia, tropical ulcers and other diseases. One evil-smelling hut, weather-beaten and very dark, was called The Death House and contained prisoners whose chances of recovery were almost nothing. It was the most depressing sight I had seen up to that time.

I was given nine quinine tablets daily, along with liver shots to combat the beriberi. My chills persisted, but since the food here was much better than that in the jungle camps, I grew steadily stronger. We could smuggle fresh fruits and vegetables from the native markets by giving the guards an outrageous cut. Dr. Epstein, one of our most respected doctors, obtained permission to permit a POW to act as agent in the purchase of special things from the native markets.

There were many men from the *Houston* and the *Perth* in the hospital. We planned a Christmas celebration, realizing that this might be our last one. Any Christmas spirit we were able to raise was promptly doused when we learned that four Aussies who had unsuccessfully attempted to escape were to be shot on Christmas Day.

No one could blame the POWs for attempting to escape. It was impossible not to spend a good deal of time plotting to escape. What did we have to lose? Months stretching into months of slave labor, the sadism of the guards, the lack of adequate clothing and food, and the almost certain opportunity of dying thousands of miles away from our families—all this made escape seem almost reasonable.

The cooler heads, however, realized that there was little chance of success in such a plan. There was the Jap army in Burma—we knew not where—600 miles of impenetrable jungle between us and the Allies, trigger-happy natives anxious for the 100 rupee price on our heads when caught outside the compound and our own debilitated condition. At the same time, we made multiple plans, only to discard them at the last moment.

The Japs chose the worst possible time for the execution. We had just sat down to Christmas dinner and had started to eat when the fusillade rang out. This day would already have been one of the saddest in our lives without this added tragedy. Gloom descended like a blanket over Thanbyuzat and we hardly knew what we ate or that we ate.

Shortly after the holidays, the guards came into our hospital hut and told us to get dressed in full uniform. We laughed outright. Since no one had even a shirt or a pair of shorts that were not in tatters, this was the most absurd order to date. In a few moments, however, medicines appeared in the usually almost bare medicine cupboards and white coats, white towels and utensils bloomed throughout the hut as though by magic.

I rubbed my eyes in disbelief.

Johnny Sayre had come down from 26 Kilo Camp with steam burns the week before. "The war's over, Jim!" he exclaimed. "You know darned well these bums wouldn't be about to give us all these things unless something really big was cooking."

"I don't think so, John," I countered. "I'll bet they've had these things all the time, to sell on the black market. During an inspection they have to produce something to make it look good."

Then an Aussie patient told us that the truckload of fresh pineapple that appeared miraculously outside the cook shack was actually a truckload of pie melon, with pineapple on top. We were wise to their scheme.

Sure enough, in a few minutes, the guards gave the order to stand by for an inspection party. When the high-ranking Jap officers had finished their tour, the guards quickly removed the medicines, coats and utensils and then returned for the uniforms. Too late, we had already traded them for food. The guards bashed us, but, for several days, we had the best meals we had had since becoming prisoners of war.

One night, while Johnny Sayre and I were speculating about our poor chances of survival, 250 new POWs arrived. They were all Americans and 50 of them were ill enough to be interned in the hospital hut. They recounted a tale of having been bombed while on a hell ship en route from Changi to Rangoon.

One ship, carrying Jap troops, had been sunk and all the Dutch on board the POW ship had been killed by bombs. Five Aussies had also lost their lives. The American patients told us about their rescue of several Jap soldiers from the water after the bombing of their ship.

One Jap soldier, however, told John and me quite a different story. "Damn Americans, no damn good!" he said, furiously. "Every time my head come up for air, damn American push it *down* again!"

The news that the Allied bombers were operating so close to the Burmese coast was a wonderful tonic.

There were many men from the *Houston* and *Perth* in the hospital camp, so we decided to hold a commemoration ceremony. I was able to discard one cane by the second week of February and on the evening of the 28th, we held the ceremony in one of the huts.

An Aussie chaplain delivered a short sermon, we sang hymns and offered a prayer. We prayed for an end to the war, for an Allied victory, for the safety of our loved ones and for a sign that we had not been forgotten.

Weeks had passed since the bombing of the Jap troopship, no planes had appeared and we had heard no encouraging news. After the service ended, gloom settled over the hut. When it grew too thick and we struggled to make light conversation, we asked John to sing.

"What should I sing?" he asked.

Seriously doubting that even Johnny's singing could raise the gloom of this occasion, I suggested he sing something inspirational, something he had not sung before during the many other sessions, almost as bad as this one, when we had asked him to sing to raise our spirits. John walked to the end of the hut. His black, curly hair had grown long and hung about his shoulders. He shook the hair back and fastened his huge, black eyes on the rafters of the hut. Barefoot, wearing patched calico shorts which he had made himself and with one arm bandaged, he sang as he had never sung before. His song was "The Bluebird of Happiness."

When he finished with the lines "So be like I, hold your head up high / You will find the bluebird of happiness." we practically brought the hut down with applause. Martinelli singing "I Pagliacci" at the Met could not have had a more appreciative audience.

Earl Scott asked us what it was like to have a ship shot from beneath us and I was elected to describe the events of that night.

"Well, everything was quiet at first," I began. "We were asleep when we came upon the Jap landing operation. Suddenly, it seemed as though heaven and hell had opened up at once. Shells poured at us from above and torpedoes from below. The darkness wasn't there anymore because of fires from the holds of the ships, searchlights and star shells.

"It was like waking up in the middle of a nightmare and not understanding what was going on, except that you knew it was disastrous and there was little you could do to change it. This went on for a while and then we were told to jump.

"We looked down into an abyss of fire, water and oil, too numb to be scared. We jumped, found a life raft, Chaplain Gray disappeared and men were dying and screaming all around us. In a little while all was quiet; the shells had stopped and the *Houston* was sinking.

"She was already covered with water, except the afterpart of the ship. Our Stars and Stripes were fluttering from the mainmast. We felt this horrible sense of loss then ... but, it's funny, we were proud, too. And now, we were scared, of course, scared of death, scared of the unknown."

I had just finished the last word when, suddenly, there was the unmistakable drone of planes. We sat immobilized for a few seconds then dashed to the doors and windows. The Japs suddenly went mad, shrieking and striking out wildly at the patients as though the devil himself had caught hold of their coattails. The huts began to shake from the vibrations of the engines. The Japs fell over each other running for the slit trenches, while the patients shouted in astonishment and delight.

"They're our planes! They're our planes!"

By this time all of the patients—at least all who could move and many who thought they couldn't and discovered they could—were outside clapping each other on the backs and yelling in wild delirium. Our prayers had been answered.

The Allied planes circled, dropped flares and dipped to within 200 feet of the tops of the huts. This was our show and they gave us our money's worth. This continued for at least 30 minutes before they departed, dropping on their way two bombs on a supply dump a short distance from the camp.

The Japs came out of the slit trenches, slowly and tentatively. If they were winning the war and the entire enemy had been killed or captured, as their newspapers stated, what planes were these? They were visibly shaken. It was also obvious that the Allied pilots knew precisely which huts quartered the POWs. They had dipped over those huts only. Twelve men had been executed for attempting to escape; therefore, Burmese agents must be sending information to the Allies. We had many friends among the natives after all.

No tonic could have done the good that the visit of the planes had accomplished. Instead of feeling we were forgotten men, condemned to die at slave labor in a steaming jungle, we suddenly felt we had a new lease on life.

Two weeks later, after having rehashed every part of the experience with the other patients, I was sent back to 26 Kilo Camp at Kun Knit Kway. Here, I relived it again and again as the POWs repeatedly requested details of the sorties.

Over and over they asked, "What happened at Thanbyuzat the night the planes came?"

It was much as a child might ask his mother to tell him about Santa Claus again and again. I told and retold the story, watching the delighted expressions of the men as the tale progressed. When I had finished many were weeping with pleasure and I doubt that they even noticed it. It brought joy where there had been despair and hope to those who no longer believed in hope.

The story of the bombing of Thanbyuzat was the only pleasant aspect of Kun Knit Kway. I was stunned to see the changes in the men since my stay in the hospital. I was given light duty carrying chow drums to the men working on the railroad. After chow in the morning, sick call was held and as the men stood in line dressed in ragged shorts, G-strings and grass sacks, I felt ill down to my toes.

There was not a single pair of healthy-looking legs in the line. Many were swollen to twice their normal size from beriberi, others were covered with tropical ulcers, ringworm, tinea and cuts and bruises. These same men who had been robust a year before were now walking skeletons with red-rimmed eyes. The entire aspect of the group was nightmarish in the extreme. After seeing them for the first time at sick call, I stopped on my trip back with the empty chow drum, sat down on a log, put my head in my hands and wept. If they had deteriorated this much in three months, it was predictable what could happen to all of us in another three months.

Every day men passed out while working on the railroad. The Japs would beat the unconscious men with their rifle butts, trying to make them get up and go back to work. When Lieutenant Simmons begged the Jap officer in charge of the camp to allow the sick men to remain in camp until they could work, he laughed in his face.

"The railroad will be *built*! Let every prisoner of war die while building it, if it is necessary!" was his comment.

We thought this represented the peak in Jap depravity, but several days later, one officer was replaced by the most hated and feared Jap officer in the jungle camp—Captain Naito, the alcoholic. We had heard many stories about him, none of them good. He was reported to be a dipsomaniac who shot prisoners without any provocation.

During the first few days we did not see him. One of the guards told Gordon Strong that he was drunk in his hut. The affect that his presence had on the guards was incredible. They usually chattered like monkeys, but since Captain Naito's arrival, they spoke only in whispers, walked about camp with furtive expressions on their faces and tried to make themselves as inconspicuous as possible.

I was put back on the *buppin* crew and went to live in a tent on the side of a hill overlooking the camp. Bob, Chuck, Tex and Marv were also on this detail. Mike and Gordon worked on the railroad. Two Englishmen completed the crew.

Knowing Captain Naito's reputation, we went to our tent immediately after evening chow each day. On the fourth day we did this as usual. We had stretched out on our platforms and had fallen asleep. Sometime near midnight we were jolted awake by a terrific commotion. We peeped out of our tent to see the guards on the tiny parade ground doing close order drill. It was not difficult to see that the small Jap officer, who was shouting curses and orders at the top of his voice in Japanese, was drunker than a hoot owl.

"That's 'im!" exclaimed one of the Englishmen. "I had 'im down the line. That's Captain Naito right enough."

Naito continued to drill the guards until they must have been on the verge of complete exhaustion. It made us tired to watch them, but at the same time, we couldn't have slept during the noise and strain. He finally yelled "*Banzai!*" and they charged into the jungle, yelling like maniacs.

When the camp finally went quiet and we returned to our bunks we were convinced that the stories about Naito were true, and that we had good reason to be apprehensive.

On the following night, Captain Naito broke out the POWs in the camp and had them move heavy railroad ties from one side of the railroad to the other. When this was accomplished he had them move the ties back where they had been originally. He ignored our tent, for which we thanked God, calling out only the men in the huts.

During the next few days he alternated guards and POWs in night drills. Then he ran out of saki and headed for Thanbyuzat.

A Christian guard named Hirowishi kept us posted on Naito's activities. He also brought us cigarettes and attempted to cheer us in any way he could. While at Thanbyuzat, Hirowishi related, Naito held a formal inspection of the entire camp at two in the morning. He kept the Allied C.O. up to watch the Jap guards drill.

When he returned to our camp he beat both the guards and the POWs, but his chief daytime chore was beating the guards. We were not the only ones with cuts and bruises now. Horseface and the Bash Artist, who had enjoyed beating us with great zeal, now bore the marks of Captain Naito.

We were wretchedly hot inside the tent and suffered from thirst. Naito refused to allow us to have water much of the time, because the creek was beginning to dry up. Our greatest worry, however, was that Dr. Hekking, who was caring for a patient who had contracted smallpox, would himself get the disease and die. He was almost our life insurance policy.

One patient of his, an Englishman, was growing worse. Large, green blow flies pestered him. Dr. Hekking told us that he picked 120 maggots out of the Englishman's pustules. When the patient lapsed into unconsciousness, Naito went berserk. He ordered the English interpreter and the Allied C.O. to move into the hut with the patient. They spent two days there before the Allied officers in camp could persuade Naito to release them.

The other POWs were moved to 14 Kilo Camp, leaving us in quarantine. Finally, the Englishman began to recover and was transferred to Thanbyuzat in a much-improved condition. We were kept in the tent for several more days then we, too, were moved to 14 Kilo Camp. No one else contracted smallpox.

Captain Naito was transferred to Thanbyuzat. Hirowishi told us some of the guards swore that they would push him down a well if he returned and started another reign of terror.

The new camp was much closer to the main camp. Perhaps that explained why we had much more food and it was in far greater variety than in the past. We also had a Japanese officer in charge who was not only efficient, but just. This was quite a phenomenon as Jap commandants in the jungle went.

He not only supplied us with more food, but punished the guards for striking us when we were obeying the rules. He also allowed us to swim in the river each day. Had this not been enough to overwhelm us, he confounded us by announcing that we would have a certain number of days off to rest up from our labors.

On the first of such days we held a Derby Day, which was enjoyed even by the Japs. Since we had no horses, we made wooden ones which were ridden by the POWs. We placed bets on these constructions and boasted about their speed, although it was obvious that no skinny POWs, impeded by heavy wooden horses, could break any records in the quarter mile race.

Everyone caught the spirit of the day. Even the Allied C.O. dressed as the "Governor" with a gaudily dressed POW clinging to his arm as the "Governor's Lady." The other officials wore bamboo top-hats and coats made of burlap bags dyed black. We also had taxi drivers, pimps and a couple of whores and all kinds of concessionaires. The latter sold rice, coffee, sandwiches, peanuts and gingerroot preserved in native sugar.

The POWs dressed as the "dates" of the others were by far the most colorful group. They had borrowed clothing from native women and appeared in a variety of costumes. One hairy POW wore only pink silk panties and rolled stockings. Chuck wore a brassiere stuffed with rags and hair made from a rope which he had unraveled. Around his waist was a colorful native sarong.

Mike wore a bright scarf around his head, a burlap bag skirt and was so heavily made up we couldn't see his freckles.

When the race had ended, boxing gloves were supplied by someone and two POWs fought to a draw. All of us hoped that there would be many more Derby Days, but this kind of treatment was too good to last and, a month later, we were transferred to 30 Kilo Camp.

CHAPTER 13

30 Kilo Camp: Creative Writing, Japanese-style

There were some redeeming features about moving to 30 Kilo Camp. The Japs were in a frenzy of preparation to prevent the success of the Allied Big Push, which they felt was imminent. Both the troops and the guards were too busy with their own worries to keep a careful eye on us, particularly in the late evening. We were able to station a guard of our own, build a small fire and discuss the news received from the two carefully hidden radios. The troops and guards spent countless hours yakking with each other, sleeping with the native women and telephoning. They had surrounded the hospital hut with pill boxes and ammunition.

"It doesn't take much imagination," I told Marv one day, "to see who'll be blown to bits when the Allies do come."

Another redeeming feature of this camp was a guard whom we called "Little George". He was a miniature Jap who frequently joined us in the evening. He brought us sugar, told us funny stories about the other guards and the officers and amused us in many ways. He was the direct antithesis of most of the guards we had encountered.

One night we were sitting around our fire when Little George appeared with his usual donation of sugar and some bananas. He was always a welcome sight.

"Why are you so nice to us, Little George?" asked Tex.

"You visit George at my home. George be real nice to big Yanks. George give sukiyaki, lotta rice and cakes."

We hooted at the idea that anyone could entertain us and try to please us by serving rice. Rice was a dirty word after a year of eating it.

Gordon, afraid George would take offense, explained what we meant and told him we would appreciate his hospitality, but would pass on the rice.

George nodded. "You be my guests. George treat alla Yanks swell. Alla Yanks from United States, California and Texas!"

I told George I had been a guest of the samurai for a year and he was the first Japanese person I had encountered who had a sense of humor.

George's round, childlike face became very serious. "George think like this." He took his right index finger and made a circle clockwise around his head, "Alla other Japs inna jungle think like this!" He made another circle counter-clockwise around his head.

We laughed. There was a good deal of truth in what he said.

"Anything new happen today?" Bob asked.

"George got slappie-slappie. My officer tell George my rifle plenty dirty. He say rifle disgrace to Imperial Army. George runna the creek and give rifle plenty good one washing. Jap officer slappie George silly, 'cause I clean my rifle!"

After we had finished laughing, George told us he was getting tired of the army. He had been asked by an NCO to bring rice cakes and tea. The NCO had been called away for a few minutes. George had waited for what he felt was long enough and then called in two POWs to eat the cakes and drink the tea. When the NCO returned George received his usual slappie-slappie.

"Tea no good cold. My friends like tea and cakes."

"Yeah, but don't you know all those bashing can scramble your brains?" asked Chuck.

"George got coconut head. Don't mind bashings. No like the samurai. Samurai thinks they winna the whole world. Samurai winna kick inna pants. Greater Asia say alla Melican planes shot down, alla British planes shot down. If this so, then you tella George what the hell planes bomb Thanbyuzat?"

Greater Asia was the propaganda newspaper, published in English in Rangoon by the Japanese. The guards delighted in waving a copy under our noses and boasting of Jap successes. One issue of the paper contained a story stating that all Allied planes had been completely destroyed. Other stories in this sheet were equally incredible.

Horseface and the Bash Artist were especially eager to recount these stories to us. One of their favorites was about a brave Japanese pilot who had found himself out of ammunition. Instead of returning to the base for more, he had "Downed the last Allied plane with rice cakes!"

Another Jap pilot who had downed all the Allied planes in one battle felt he should do something else to show his great affection for the Emperor. He had swooped his plane low enough over an American warship to decapitate the captain with his samurai sword.

The paper gave outrageous figures for Allied losses. We always assumed the stated Allied losses were actually Japanese and the Japanese losses were those sustained by the Allies.

One reporter told how the elephants in Burma were so pleased with the Japanese for freeing them from the cruel British that they had stood in line and, lifting their trunks, had "Let forth a resounding trumpet of salutation in honor of their deliverers, the heroic Imperial Army whom they loved." The Japs habitually starved and mistreated the elephants, much as they did the POWs. We felt sorry for the beasts and even sorrier for ourselves because we could not use the huge beasts for food when they dropped dead from overwork and mistreatment. We felt we might soon join the dead ones.

Horseface did not understand much American slang and idioms left him cold. His special self-imposed assignment appeared to be making our quite unpleasant lot even more untenable. One day he came to us boasting that eight prostitutes had been imported for the amusement of the guards. We had seen the sad-eyed, worn-looking girls and had felt sorry for them, particularly in view of the fact that they had to amuse Horseface.

"We have wonderful time with prostitutes," he boasted. "You got no women!"

"Damned if I'll ever be that hard up!" snorted Chuck.

"Our libido doesn't give us much trouble. We're more interested in food," I told Horseface.

Since he didn't understand what libido meant, he was immediately affronted, feeling he had lost face in front of us. He produced his most malignant glare and turned it on us full force. When it became obvious that we didn't think very highly of his prostitutes—and were not concerned that we had been left out—he switched to his supercilious look and told us in icy tones that we did not know what we were missing.

"You go ahead and enjoy them, sonny," drawled Tex, "We set our sights a little higher than you do."

Horseface flew into a rage and screamed at us: "Japan win war! Amelica no planes, no fleet! Soon Japanese do this to prisoners!" He stopped stomping about, clicked the heels of his boots together and made a motion of cutting his throat with his right hand.

He extracted a sheet from *Greater Asia* and threw it at my feet. This one, too, recounted the brave exploits of Jap pilots. One in particular had had his plane shot down the middle. Grievously wounded, the brave pilot had landed the plane, fought his way through countless miles of jungle, in order to report at last to his senior officer back at his base.

On the morning of May 20, we were awakened as usual by Horseface with his wooden clappers. I suddenly sat straight up and listened. Rain! It was here! I looked at Gordon in despair. Rain meant a death notice to many of the sick, perhaps to all of us. Rain was what we had dreaded most. It meant no Big Push until after the rainy season. It took little imagination to visualize what would happen to men as debilitated as we were if we were forced to continue to live under the existing conditions.

Horseface, sensing our low morale because of the rain, decided to needle us about Allied losses. We tried to ignore him and went to our details. When we returned for noon chow he began once more. The rain was not yet heavy, but showers were falling.

Suddenly, we heard the steady drone of planes. "Japanese planes!" said Horseface, smugly.

Jap planes came over every day en route to Rangoon or Thailand. We stood in line, mess gear in hand, most of us not even bothering to look skyward.

Bob McCann stood directly in front of me, looking up at the planes.

"Better put your head down, Bob," Marv teased. "Don't you know snub-nosed people never look up when it's raining?"

Bob didn't answer immediately, but suddenly let out a whoop that galvanized the lot of us. He threw his mess gear into the air and began beating me on the back as though he had "gone out of his gourd," as Chuck would say.

All along the line more mess gear sailed into the air, and POWs screeched in a frenzy of delight. Horseface took one look and dove into a slit trench. Directly overhead were six of the most beautiful, four-engined planes that America ever produced!

Every Jap in sight ran for the bush or a slit trench, while the POWs danced, shrieked, laughed and wept in sheer delight. The planes were headed toward Thanbyuzat and in a short while we heard the *boom! boom!* of falling bombs hitting some target.

After a while, we ate our lunch and the Japs straggled back, looking quite sheepish. They had abandoned their rifles in their haste and were picking them up. That afternoon we went to our details with the first real smile we had mustered for months. For many of the men, these were the first Allied planes they had sighted in the jungle and the sight of something marked "Made in the U.S.A." was better than many bottles of medicine.

On the following day planes appeared again, this time dropping bombs near our camp. At the first glimpse of them the Japs scrambled for the ditches or the brush, falling all over each other in their haste. I regret to say that the sight of terror on the faces of our captors gave us almost as much pleasure as the appearance of the planes.

Horseface and his cohorts were frightened and irritable. They swore at us and told us repeatedly that the planes would never dare repeat their performance, because the Japanese would shoot them down. The Japs not only did not shoot them down, but the planes appeared overhead almost every day. The guards and soldiers almost stopped trying to explain it. They could not understand why the planes came when *Greater Asia* continually told them that there were no more American planes. We had a respite from having them throw the propaganda newspaper into our faces, but their irritability only increased. They were confused and angry. This took nothing away from our delight. Each time the planes appeared we sang, danced and literally jumped for joy. Our morale soared.

Then word came down the line that greatly diminished our joy, or at least made us look at these new developments in a more serious light, such being the effect they could have on our lives. Lieutenant Simmons returned from Thanbyuzat. In the first bombing 14 men had been killed outright, the Allied C.O. had narrowly escaped death and his assistant had been fatally injured. Fifty patients had been seriously injured and later succumbed to their wounds. Many of these men were our friends from the *Houston* and the *Perth* and we felt their loss keenly. It was too ironic—too tragic—that these men should survive all the brutal treatment and the general misery the Japs could dish out—even the horror of the hell ships—only to meet death from our own bombers.

On the day we received this news, Chuck's legs became so bad from beriberi that he had to remain in camp and serve as "dog-robber" or personal servant-valet to the Jap guards. He cleaned their huts, washed their clothing and did other disagreeable tasks.

After one day of this we returned from our *buppin* and railroad building details to find him practically apoplectic with fury. "I'll grab one of their rifles and shoot myself before I'll work another day on this shitting detail. No self-respectin' gyrene would be caught dead being a wet nurse to these slant-eyed bastards!"

The veins on his forehead stood out like purple cords, his sandy hair flying sixty ways for Sunday. He stomped back and forth like a caged animal. Watching him pull at his cauliflower ear I thought he was on the verge of one of his famous blow-ups, and I was right. He suddenly picked up the bamboo platform that served as his bunk and threw it against the wall of the hut, where it crashed into dozens of bamboo splinters.

The noise brought the Bash Artist on the run. Instead of whipping to attention at the sight of the guard, Chuck doubled up both huge tattooed fists and moved slowly and menacingly toward the Jap, while I said a prayer that he would not get into trouble.

The Bash Artist looked confused and frightened. He was at a disadvantage since he did not know what had started the commotion. We later decided that he had thought Chuck had gone berserk, since mental illness was on the rise among the POWs. All the Japs were intensely fearful of anyone with mental disease.

The Bash Artist stood like a wooden statue, not even trying to lift his gun. He seemed powerless to move, his eyes glued on the irate, glowering prisoner. As Chuck slowly and steadily approached, he bumped into a heavy wooden table. Picking it up in one strong hand and without looking back, he flung it completely through the wall of the hut.

Simultaneously, a frightened, furious Little George burst through the door of the hut, gesticulating frantically. "Stoppa damn God mucha noise! Don't you fool Big Yanks know Captain Naito back?" he hissed.

Fortunately, Naito was drunk again and, if he had heard the noise, he was too inebriated to function. The Bash Artist left with Little George.

We repaired the hole in the hut in double time as quietly as possible. Gordon and I begged an empty bamboo platform from one of the native bungs. It was full of lice and bedbugs, but so were we. As Bob McCann expressed it: a few wild parasites to join the tame ones we had would make smarter siblings than either group of parents.

"As a matter of fact," he went on, "no damn smart bedbug or louse will hang around this bunch of skinny POWs unless it plans to starve to death, too!"

"They're gonna give up soon, anyway," Mike predicted. "My pa always said you can't get blood out of a turnip and, goodness knows, we ain't got much more blood left than a durned turnip!" Mike, too, had beriberi and, in addition, his legs were horribly mutilated by tropical ulcers. Two days later he was sent to the main hospital camp at Thanbyuzat.

We didn't feel it was wise to leave Chuck for another day as dog-robber. Lieutenant Simmons got permission for us to take him on the *buppin* detail. He was hardly able to walk the distance to the wood-cutting, but once there we made him sit on a log while we stuffed him with the celery-like bamboo shoots, pomelos and anything else that was both green and edible. As a result of the rest and the fresh fruits and "vegetables," he was soon much improved.

Captain Naito called the guards out for a midnight drill three nights after his return to 30 Kilo Camp at Retpu but after that he seemed strangely quiet. One night, a Dutchman, on his way to the latrine, found the captain standing by the latrine. He appeared to be very depressed and told the prisoner that Italy was near surrender, that Germany was almost defeated and that Japan would have to fight the whole world alone.

Although this made Naito sad, it had the reverse effect on us. After that night, however, Naito scarcely had a sober minute. He found another

Dutchman at the latrine a few nights later and shot him in the abdomen without a word of warning. The POW did not die, although it was close.

The maniac captain walked the compound every night with drawn pistol and none of us dared to go out. Since many of the dysentery patients could not adjust to this schedule and had to use pails in the huts, this made it quite unbearable for all.

Allied planes continued to bomb supply dumps, railroads, anti-aircraft centers—and we lived in constant fear that 30 Kilo would be next. The order came to evacuate Thanbyuzat. A truck was provided for 50 of the most critically ill patients, but about 3,000 others were told to take their gear and march into the jungle to 30 Kilo Camp, almost 30 miles away.

The greater proportion of these patients had not walked a step for months. They were sent into the jungle without food, water, medicine or clothing. To have shot them would have been more humane, since many of them were either mental cases, blind, or both. No provision for any shelter was provided, even though it was the rainy season.

They fell like ninepins along the road and many were unable to rise after the first collapse. Some trekked to the first camp at 8 Kilo, but those in the most serious condition did not progress beyond a few yards. Only a handful arrived at the prescribed destination.

We could hardly believe it when we saw what looked like a group of skeletons lurching and crawling through the mud toward camp. One of these was Mike Sullivan, almost blind from beriberi, who told us he could not use the road and had managed to crawl from Thanbyuzat by feeling his way from tree to tree along the road.

The march had hardly begun when the rains came down in earnest and dozens of patients with high fevers, many delirious and completely disoriented, stumbled and slipped, falling into the mire.

We looked with horror at these wraiths with death-mask faces, open, muddy wounds, and horribly swollen, bleeding legs. Some had cards fastened to them stating in both Japanese and English that they were blind or insane. Many of the cards, however, had been lost in their struggle through the muddy jungle.

We took them in at once and scrambled about getting platforms, food and cleaning their wounds. There was some satisfaction in having even these few patients under our care, where we felt we could try to save them. No single act of the Japs did more to show us how callous they could be toward the sick. They seemed to be devising ways to make sure as many of us as possible would perish before the Allies arrived.

The Japs made our work doubly hard by ordering all patients out into the jungle in the pouring rain, from ten in the morning until late in the afternoon. This largely undid what we had managed to do to improve the health of those on the forced march from Thanbyuzat.

The Japs were shocked out of their smug complacency about winning the war by the regular bombing missions of the Allied planes. They told us that the prisoners must accompany them into the jungle to prevent their escape. It was absurd to assume that any of these poor half-demented men could escape from anything.

There was one bright aspect of the jungle treks, however—we were able to obtain food from the native *camponga* scattered about the camp.

Regardless of bombs, rain and anything else that transpired, Captain Naito continued his reign of terror. The Allied bombings only made him more unpredictable. He never drew a sober breath from the day the missions assumed some form of regularity.

One night he took a Dutch prisoner from his hut, made him dig his grave and shot him in the back. A guard at the graveside tripped the Dutch prisoner and Naito's other shots went wild. The Dutchman rose to his feet and ran screaming into one of the huts where the other POWs hid him. In all fairness to the guards, they knew precisely where the fugitive was, but they didn't turn him over to the maniac captain.

After several more days and nights of terror, Hirowishi, realizing that something must be done, slipped from camp without permission and met Nagatomo, who was on his way to 30 Kilo Camp. Hirowishi reported Naito's activities to the commandant. Nagatomo arrived in camp just in time to see Naito in a drunken frenzy beating up two Jap engineers. He ordered Naito trussed and thrown into the back of truck. Naito was taken to the hospital at Moulmein, where he was allowed no alcohol, including his sacred saki wine.

All of the guards got drunk that night and told us to have a concert. Naito's replacement was a more circumspect specimen.

CHAPTER 14

64 Kilo Camp: Jesus Wept

In September we moved deeper into the jungle to 64 Kilo Camp. We made the trip on foot, wading in mud almost to our knees. The last 200 yards was traversed on a catwalk across a swollen river. Tex, Chuck, Gordon, John and I carried 200-pound rice sacks on our backs.

I thought of my brother Ben, who had always admired anyone who could carry a 100-pound sack of anything and wondered what he would think of the spectacle we made crossing the rampaging river, in pouring rain, clad only in G-strings. At least we were not burdened with clothing. A sudden downpour, more severe than usual, began to shake the catwalk and I began to wonder if we would ever make it to the other side. The wind shrieked, the rain lashed our bare skin, the catwalk bounced, and all about us every shrub and blade of grass in sight formed its own water spout from the buckets of rain.

When we finally arrived at the new camp on the other side I wanted to go back to 30 Kilo. I took one look at the dead natives lying about, their bodies in various stages of decomposition, the waist-high weeds, the fallen huts and the native excrement and felt ill.

We set about burying the natives, building pit latrines and constructing new huts. John and the other cooks attempted to start fires, but the wet wood smoked, driving them from the cook shack. John kept running out of the shack, rubbing his eyes and cursing. He practically never used profanity, but the provocation was great. We were all ravenously hungry, having had no food throughout the day. We were bone-weary from our long trek through the mud and the rain and there were still long hours of work ahead of us.

We needed no one to tell us that it would be extremely difficult to get food to this remote camp. In our struggle to reach it we had seen large sections of railroad that had been bombed out or washed out, bombed bridges and many signs that the Allies were making it difficult for the enemy to perform its conquest of the world.

When we discovered that the Jap sergeant in charge of the camp loathed all white men with an intensity that bordered on the maniacal we realized we had other problems. He immediately cut our rice ration to a tablespoon per day. The medical staff consisted of a two-star private and a veterinarian, who offered no objections when the sergeant ordered the dysentery patients (many of whom were dying) out into the pouring rain for *tenko*. All of them were stretcher cases who took two POWs to carry. Fortunately, some of the patients were already in a coma.

It was no surprise to any of us that the little attap morgue was soon filled to overflowing. We lost six patients the first week and, by the end of the month, three or four POWs were dying daily. As I passed the morgue to help dig graves, a voice seemed to say, "When will you come?" to which the geckos croaked their agreement as I dug the graves.

One day, an Englishman on the grave-digging detail got a splinter in his hand. He died within the week. We had no resistance to disease left.

My malaria returned and, three days out of seven, I was down with chills and a high fever. By the end of the second month, seven or more men were dying daily. I wondered who would be digging my grave.

Tex was taken off the *buppin* crew to help me dig graves. The increase in the number of deaths kept us busy. When the requisite graves were finished for the day, we were told to carry the 30-gallon water drums from the river to the cook shack, where the water was boiled. We slipped, slid and fell in the mud many times. Often, I wondered whether I should get up or just remain sprawled where I had fallen. It required little skill to keep standing while digging the graves, but to stay in an upright position while carrying the enormous drums was a feat worthy of a tightrope walker.

One particularly rainy, dismal day, Tex and I were carrying the unwieldy drum up the hillside when he slipped, falling flat on his face in the mud. The water cascaded over him and the trail behind us. Tex had his own expressions for situations of this type. He lay on his belly, spitting the mud out of his mouth. I expected some choice profanity when he was finally able to talk, but he raised one mud-smeared eyebrow and recited, in a singsong voice: "Jesus wept and Moses crept and Peter went a-fishin."

A heard a low whistle behind us and a deep voice with a heavy Dutch accent said, "That's the biggest gecko I've ever seen, in or out of the mud. They're getting larger every day. They'll be taking advantage of us soon!"

It was Dr. Hekking! I let the other handle of the heavy drum fall from my fingers and the huge container bounced down the hill. I made no effort to stop the flow of tears that gushed down my cheeks. I wanted to see no man in the world more than I wanted to see him—not even my own father. I knew it would cause my father great sorrow to see me in the present physical condition, but the arrival of Doc Hekking meant that many of my friends in the hospital would survive. When he finished pouring his magic herb concoctions down their throats, men who had weeks ago decided to die would be back on the railroad detail.

We detained him only long enough to express our joy, knowing the sight of him was a great tonic for the patients in the death hut. As we walked with him to the hut, we explained how most of us had lost hope, how the stench from the tropical ulcers alone made us hold our noses when we passed the hospital hut. When we had shown him where the patients' hut was we returned for the water and to allow Tex to wash some of the mud away.

While Tex was washing, we looked up to see a stream of POWs walking along the catwalk toward our camp. One of these was Captain Morgan, looking pale and gaunt, but apparently still able to get about under his own power. Tex and I went to meet him hoping to hear some good news of Mike, since both had been patients in 55 Kilo.

Before we reached him he waved one arm and yelled, "Guess you heard your sidekick Mike Sullivan croaked!"

Both Tex and I stood perfectly still. Both of us were stunned by both the news and the way he had conveyed it. Morgan still wore his smirk, but the carefully trimmed mustache of Batavia days looked like an overgrown weed patch. I didn't look at Tex, but I knew he was having a terrible struggle with himself to keep from pushing this miserable excuse for an officer backward into the rampaging, muddy river behind him.

After Morgan had gone, Tex sat for a long while staring into the muddy river. When the rain began to lash about us in sheets, he picked up his handle of the heavy water drum and we proceeded with heavy hearts toward camp. That evening, Bob, Gordon, Tex and I took turns whittling a wooden cross to serve as a marker for Mike's grave. We sent it by the next truck driver to 55 Kilo Camp, knowing that our friends there would see that it would be placed where it belonged.

Two weeks later Gordon came rushing into the hospital hut, where I was recovering from a bout of malaria, and startled us with the statement that Horseface had just died.

"You must be delirious, Gordon!" I raised myself on one elbow and felt his forehead for fever. The red hair was growing sparser, but the high brow beneath my fingers was cool.

"I know it's incredible, but the Bash Artist told me and he's petrified. He said the Japanese have the best food, medicine and warm clothing and there is no reason why anyone in His Imperial Majesty's Army should die from disease."

Horseface was indeed dead. He had died from dysentery. The other Japs went about with drawn, frightened faces. The Jap sergeant called for volunteers to build a funeral pyre for Horseface and every POW who could lift a small stick turned out to help.

"Why you want such hard work?" asked the Bash Artist, visibly perplexed, as the POWs went about cutting down trees and gathering wood for the fire. He had never seen the prisoners perform any chore with such gusto.

"I reckon you wouldn't understand!" said Tex and we left it there.

Food—quantities of rice and fruits—were carefully arranged about the funeral pyre, gasoline was poured over the wood and the whole ignited. The Japs stood sadly about while the body was cremated. Then the Bash

Artist carefully picked small pieces of bone from the ashes and put them in a box covered with a white cloth and bearing a brass name plate. All that remained of Horseface would be sent back to Japan.

I recalled that only a few days before he had stood over the grave I was digging and boasted of Japanese successes. The Burmese, he told us, had joined the Japanese against the Allies. This, he told Tex and me, would make the war end quickly, because the Great Army of Burma was one the Allies could fear with good reason. This boast had been particularly irritating to us because it was so very ludicrous. We had visual proof of the state of the poor Burmese.

All about the camp lay the decomposing bodies of the natives. We had buried the first ones when we came to camp, but those that had since died were left where they fell. We repeatedly asked the Japs to allow us to bury the poor bungs, but they refused. Starving, wretched mothers sat beneath streaming palm trees, many with dead babies in their arms. Tiny children with matchstick legs and the bloated abdomens of the underfed drifted from corpse to corpse wailing in a high, faint voice for any kind of food. Hardly a day passed that we did not see an old Burmese beaten or kicked to death because he asked for food or medicine for his starving family.

Three days after the demise of Horseface another guard succumbed to dysentery and the funeral pyre was again lit. Not since the days of Naito had we seen the guards so frightened. We were as puzzled as they as to the reason for the deaths, until one day, while Tex was passing the cook shack, he heard the POW cooks discussing the guards.

"Sometimes I think the guards drive them right up the wall, boasting about their successes when the poor guys are starving to death. The only good Jap is a dead Jap."

"Yep and it's time we had another good one."

"Go ahead!"

With this, the cook picked up a dead rat from the back of the cook shack and dipped it into a plate of stew dished up for the guards. In a few days, another guard's ashes were shipped to Japan.

There were also reports that the cooks stirred the bowel movements of the dysentery patients into the Japs' supper, but this we could not believe. Johnny Sayre was horrified when we quizzed him about it. He insisted he had never seen the cooks do anything to make the Japs sick and we believed him. But, the fact remained that Tex had seen the episode of the rat.

Despite Dr. Hekking's best efforts, without food his work was doubly difficult and the number of deaths rose to an appalling figure. All of us had sores inside our mouths and on our genital organs. He told us these were from pellagra, another indicator of malnutrition. Bob's throat became covered with sores and he could no longer talk. The best he could do was to make a croaking sound.

The only time we had a piece of meat in the stew was when an ox dropped dead from starvation. Some of the POWs were always on the lookout for one that was beginning to falter and, when it finally collapsed in the mud, the butchers—with a whoop of glee—fell upon it and cut its throat.

My malaria refused to respond to quinine. Finally, Dr. Hekking gave me an intravenous injection which he said had an arsenic base. Not only did the symptoms disappear, but I had no recurrence of the disease.

We worried as much about Dr. Hekking as we worried about ourselves. He showed a selfless devotion to the sick. Night after night he sat by the besides of the desperately ill patients, encouraging them, caring for them and telling them they were going to get well. When all else failed to cheer them, he took a small black book from his pocket. This famous book was filled with jokes: English jokes, Aussie jokes, American jokes and Dutch jokes. Read by Dr. Hekking, with his thick Dutch accent, they brought laughs from the most despondent of his patients. Many parents whose sons survived the rigors of a Japanese prison camp owe this fine doctor a debt of gratitude for saving the lives of their sons.

Three times Dr. Hekking had saved my life. I had been spared in the sinking of the *Houston*—in the battles that had preceded it—in the trip on the hell ship and twice in the jungle. Bob said it was Luck, Marv called it Fate and Gordon called it Faith and the working of a Divine plan. Who was right? I was surrounded by death and the dying. I could close my eyes and see the corpses of the POWs waiting for me to do one last chore for them. All about me were gaunt, walking skeletons, some of whom went down for the last time. Daily life was a severe testing of mental, moral and physical strength and I couldn't see how it could go on much longer.

Bad as conditions were in our camp, I soon learned that they were worse in others. Piece by piece, we were hearing the story of what was taking place across the border in Thailand. As the railroad crept deeper and deeper into the jungle and closer and closer to Thailand, truck drivers, POWs, guards and Jap soldiers brought bits of news about an especially unfortunate branch of POWs. These men made up the group which was forced by the Japs to make the infamous Burma Railway death march. They were driven day after day beneath a scorching, blistering sun or in pouring, lashing rain, without food, rest, medicine or any kind of shelter. They were ill, wounded, some with raging fevers, some with badly infected wounds and fractured limbs. Guards beat them for not keeping up, regardless of whether or not they had two good legs on which to stand; their captors delighted in striking them with rifle butts directly on the wounds themselves. Perishing from thirst, they finally drank from contaminated water and contracted cholera and dysentery. Then they died like animals along the way. Those who survived the 200-mile trek arrived in the jungle just in time to be caught in the rains. In their debilitated condition, this was mass murder. There were not enough healthy men left to dig the graves for the dead.

Out of a force of 10,000 who began the march, 4,000 soon succumbed to the impossible conditions imposed upon them. The Japs ordered a fire pit dug and kept burning day and night. Into this it were thrown the steadily increasing number of corpses of the Allied prisoners of war.

Chuck's fierce hatred of the oppressor seemed to sustain him. It kept him going when he might have given up the struggle. With the return of Captain Morgan, another cocklebur was jammed under Chuck's saddle. We had the old problem of keeping his hatred from erupting into violence.

Sometimes I thought he delighted in keeping us guessing about his intentions. One morning we were packing our gear for a trip deeper into the jungle when he looked at me, rubbed his hands together and said, "Oh, Boy!" in a mysterious way. I looked at his huge, bony hands, thinking how strange they looked after the long months of near starvation. Only the blue eagle tattooed on the back of his right one assured me that they were the same pair of hands.

"I can't for the life of me see why you're so happy to be moving, Chuck," I told him, "particularly since the new camp is the one where all those Englishmen died of cholera."

"I might get an opportunity to do something that would please me almost as much as watching that Jap out there drown in the river."

I dropped the gear I was packing and dashed outside. POWs were streaming toward the river bank. A Jap sergeant stood on the muddy bank yelling hysterically in Japanese. We hurried as fast as we could, slipping and sliding in the mud.

The river was a muddy torrent of swirling currents and lashing foam. About ten yards out, fighting desperately but losing the battle, was the Bash Artist. I had never seen a Jap as completely terrified as our old enemy was at that moment.

"Good God, somebody had better pull him out!" shrieked Morgan, excitedly. "The fool will drown!"

"Go right ahead and save him, captain," Chuck suggested and added, "I don't swim so well myself."

"Who's a good swimmer?" asked Lieutenant Simmons. "That river is playing for keeps."

"Out of the way! Clear the decks!" yelled Marv, trying to push his way through the crowd. We had almost forgotten that he had won every kind of trophy for his swimming prowess. He plunged into the wild river and began swimming with swift, sure strokes toward the drowning man.

Despite Marv's weakened condition, he successfully fought the raging river and dragged the spent Jap to shore. While we congratulated Marv, the wildly chattering Japs took the Bash Artist into a hut and dried him off.

In a few minutes the Japanese sergeant walked into our hut with an envelope in his hand. "Honorable Japanese wish big Yank have pay for saving his life," he said with an air of importance. He handed the envelope to Marv, who tore it open, holding the contents out in the palm of his hand. It was a bright and shiny fifty cent piece.

Marv thanked the Jap sergeant with much solemnity and, after he was gone, we roared with laughter. "Well," said Marv, shrugging his shoulders, "that's just about what the Bash Artist is worth."

There was the unmistakable sound of planes and we rushed outside again, this time to see six huge American planes outlined against the now blue sky. The rains were ending! Now there was nothing to stop The Big Push. The planes bombed the railroad only a short distance away, while the Japs, caught by surprise, ran frantically into the jungle, leaving their guns behind. They were so intent on saving their own skins, they had momentarily forgotten about the prisoners.

We were surprised to be taken to the new camp by train. The railroad crossed deep ravines, often spanned by a shaky wooden bridge, supported by beams thrust into the clefts of the rocky walls. We continued deep into Thailand, acutely aware that we traveled over a railroad that had been built at a horrible cost in human lives.

At the new camp there were fresh vegetables, which we fell upon at once, determined to rid ourselves of the pellagra sores that tormented us. There were also fat snakes which we chased and cooked, delighted to have some scraps of meat to enliven our ever-present rice.

There was always a tragic incident, however, to mar our pleasure with improved conditions. An English POW pursued a snake to the riverbank. It was large and fat and, having been long without meat, he was quite zealous in his pursuit. It took refuge in a bush and he tried to dislodge it by shaking the bush. He was promptly bitten, swelled up and died within 24 hours.

There were pleasant incidents, too. Bob's croaking voice, which had persisted for months, rendering conversations with him all but impossible, returned with a startling suddenness. He had been troubled by recurring attacks of malaria for several months. But, on a particular night, we were sound asleep when we were abruptly awakened by shouting.

"Air raid! Air raid! Hit the deck flares! Get out of here!"

The shouting was so urgent and our nerves in such a poor state that Gordon and I found ourselves outside in a ditch before we had time to assess why we were there. Marv, equally excited, went through the side of the attap hut, head first. As we lay there waiting for the sound of planes which never came, it finally occurred to us that it had been the voiceless Bob who had been shouting due to delirium from the malaria. We went back into the hut to investigate, delighted that he could talk, but, when we tried to congratulate him, he started the yelling again.

Gordon and I sat up the remainder of the night trying to convince him that the air raid was a figment of his imagination. As soon as the Chinese cooks arose to cook the rice, we bought some quinine pills from them and gave him several doses during the day.

That night we slept peacefully, but on the following night Morgan, fully recovered from dysentery but down with malaria and a high fever, became delirious. A tall tree rose above his bed. The hut had been constructed around the tree and, in his delirium, the captain was convinced that his family had arrived by plane and were in the top of the tree. He talked to them unceasingly for two nights and two days before we were able to obtain enough quinine from the Chinese cooks to combat the malaria. The cooks had many kinds of drugs, but their prices were quite prohibitive and at that this stage we had little money. Even Chuck, however, despite his antipathy for the officer, shelled out his share of money for the quinine.

After only a few weeks we were loaded into cattle cars and taken to another camp, arriving near midnight after a journey that took almost 20 hours. We were unloaded at a railroad station in Kanburi, where, despite the late hour, we were met by a reception committee of the healthiest-appearing group of POWs whom I had seen since Batavia days.

We were escorted to the new camp and served a meal that made all of us feel we must surely be dreaming. There was pork, rice, beans, bean sprouts, eggs and an assortment of green plants mixed together and fried. We had arrived at the rehabilitation camp and, as soon as we had regained our strength, would be returned to the jungle to repair the damage done to the railroad by the Allied bombing raids. The strongest of the group would be sent to Japan to work in the coal mines.

Every meal seemed like Thanksgiving.

"They are fattening us for the kill!" Bob predicted.

"Bob, I believe you'd be astounded if you survived this war," I told him.

He agreed and went on to ask me if I had noticed that the Japs were frightened of the Siamese, the Thais. "The Siamese gals take nothing off of the Japs. Every time one looks cross at the Nips, they give her a gift."

"Yesterday," I said, "the cooks complained to me that they ran out of wood because the Siamese gal in charge of the men made them stack it in crooked ricks. The piles looked larger than they actually were. I complained to the Siamese woman selling the wood. She reported me to the Jap commandant and he came trotting over to see her with a box of candy and some flowers."

"The Siamese hate the Nips," Gordon commented. "They sabotage them every chance they get."

It was a fact. The Japs were always instructing us to watch the Siamese for evidence of sabotage. We considered this quite a joke.

The rains ceased altogether and Jap troops began to pour through Thailand. Others were returned from the front wounded and, at the sight of these, the Japs guards became extremely dejected.

On June 5, about 1000, we were going about our chores when we heard the roar of planes. It sounded like the entire Allied air force was approaching Kanburi—or could it be the Japs? Since it was King George VI's birthday, and at the first roar of the planes the Japs dove for the air-raid shelters, we assumed the planes must be ours. The Japs had ordered us inside our huts but, as they did not stick around to enforce the order, we were slow in complying. We watched the sky, hoping to see the planes in passing. We didn't have long to wait before we were well rewarded. At least fifty B-29s and B-17s roared over the camp. Our jaws dropped at the sight of the B-29s, since we had never seen one before: they were enormous!

The planes remained in the area for at least half an hour, flying low and stunting. The result of this, as far as we were concerned, was an elation that defied description. The Japs were worried, frightened and irritable. After they had had an opportunity to assess the seriousness of the situation, one of the NCOs gave us the pleasant news that they had orders to machine-gun all POWs the minute an Allied landing on the Japanese mainland appeared imminent. We interpreted this to mean that Japan seemed on the verge of losing the war. Nothing they could say could dampen our spirits, however. They had never before intimated to us that there was the slightest possibility that the Japanese might lose the war.

After some months spent at Kanburi, the doctors could find nothing wrong with me except a few remaining tropical ulcers on my legs. I had a constant backache, but this they attributed to my having carried too many 200-pound rice sacks.

On July 4, we were sent to Singapore to be quartered in filthy huts occupied by Aussie and British POWs—and by Gurkhas. We were amused to find that the Japanese were deathly afraid of the latter. They even permitted the Gurkhas to take their meals in the same restaurants in which the Japanese were served.

Our current detail was to loot the beautiful homes in Singapore and to load practically everything of value on ships bound for Japan. This was the first opportunity we had had since Batavia to pick up items which could be traded for food, drugs and sometimes money.

We were awakened each morning by the vomiting of the Gurkhas. It was a ritual: they vomited each morning before they ate. They also sang and chanted in their temple. This sometimes lasted all night and was accompanied by the unremitting beat of a tom-tom. We soon became accustomed to this and, tired from the long day's labor, slept through the noise.

Bob, Tex and Marv adopted the Gurkha haircut, shaving their heads except for a long pigtail which Gurkhas believed would be used to lift them to heaven. They showed us their vicious-looking knives, kukris, then pricked their fingers to draw blood before returning the knives to the place of concealment. Their taboo forbade their replacing the knife without drawing blood. This made us shiver.

Near the end of September we went to work at Jeep Island, where we toiled in the mud 14 hours each day while Japanese officers, wearing white gloves and white uniforms, sat on the bluff at the top of the pit beneath umbrellas, smoking cigarettes. Bob called them the monkeys in the peanut gallery.

In November, Dutch POWs replaced us. They were to finish the excavation of a huge pit being dug. A dry dock was to be constructed for the Nips.

Back in Singapore, we learned from Lieutenant Simmons that an Aussie colonel had confided that he was an agent. He had the facts and was not guessing. What he told Lieutenant Simmons gave us a new lease on life. He assured him that Japan was effectively blockaded by Allied submarines, the Battle of Burma was being won by our troops; the British had a fleet in the Indian Ocean and the greatest landing force in the history of the world was en route to the Philippines.

The Japs dimmed our delight somewhat by announcing that we would leave for Japan on December 1. We were thrilled by the news of Allied progress, but had no illusions about another trip on a Jap hell ship. It seemed reasonable to assume that our chances of being bombed by our own forces were far greater than they had been previously.

CHAPTER 15

Kyushu Coal-mining

A new POW arrived in camp. He was an American Air Force colonel who had bailed out over Burma and been taken prisoner by the Japs. He had more information for us, some of which was almost unbelievable. He told us that the Philippines would soon fall to Allied forces, that the U.S. Navy had a hundred aircraft carriers, that the war would last another year and that—and this was most incomprehensible to all of us—the U.S. Armed Forces now had women, both officers and enlisted personnel, who were not nurses, but were called WAVEs, WACs, SPARs and USMCWs, female marines.

"How come a couple thousand of these gals aren't POWs?" Marv wanted to know, at once.

"How," asked John, "do you make love to them in a cruddy uniform?"

"Never mind about that, son, just lead me to them! I can take care of a little problem like that!" This from Tex.

"Maybe they could show us how to cook this damned wormy rice—so's it'd taste like chow instead of shit," Chuck snorted.

The date set for our departure finally arrived. The Jap cargo ship waited in the harbor. We prepared to go aboard. One thousand POWs were loaded, then we were told there was no room for more. We must wait for the next ship. The only American in this first group was the Air Force colonel.

Several days later, we learned, to our horror, that the ship had been sunk. Only 89 POWs had survived. This convinced all of us, except

Gordon, that we could expect to lose our lives. Morale was so low that no one even tried to raise it. This was too much. Had we survived all those grueling years of prison camp only to be bombed or torpedoed by our own side?

Once more we exchanged names of relatives, wrote short messages and secretly despaired of ever seeing the States again. I believe that my feeling of resentment was greater than it had been during any of the previous periods of danger. I wanted to see my family again, to have an opportunity to marry my girl. I was not ready to die. At the same time, I told myself that Mike Sullivan had been full of life and the desire to live, as had the Air Force colonel and they were both dead.

On December 14 we were given a brown, woolen British uniform, a woolen undershirt, a pair of Japanese cotton shorts and half of a woolen rug looted from a Singapore home. We were told to turn in any money to be exchanged for Japanese currency. The shocked faces of Japanese officials were something to see when 750 POWs turned in $21,600.

The boarding of the hell ship was uneventful. A dousing rain wet us to the skin before we were finally aboard. Being wet did nothing to raise our spirits, nor did the sight of a gaping torpedo hole in the bow of the ship.

We settled ourselves as best we could in the bottom of the hold, constantly rearranging ourselves to accommodate the stretcher cases brought aboard. These were men suffering from dysentery and malaria. Then came assorted cargo, chiefly tin and rubber that shared the hold with us.

And we waited and waited and waited. The ship stayed in port. Finally, even Gordon began to worry, not about our eventual fate, but about the mood of the group.

"There's something different about this trip, Jim. The fellows usually gripe and tease and joke, but they aren't doing that this time. They're too quiet. We know how dangerous hell ships are. We know that the Japs will close that single hatch opening if there is an air raid. Why don't the guys sound off? They're too stoical, they're trying to hide their misery."

I agreed. It was a bad sign.

Christmas Day found us still waiting. The Nips served us a feast that consisted of boiled cabbage, dehydrated boiled potatoes and a small piece of some kind of meat. This comparatively elaborate meal gave us enough strength to allow us to sing Christmas carols.

John was just starting "Adeste Fidelis" when a guard promptly appeared and complained that the noise was disturbing to the ships' captain.

On the following morning, the *Awa Maru* got underway. Rain began to fall in torrents, the sea roared, the ship dipped and the Japs bellowed at us and at each other. Most of us were pale green in color, but we did not stop praying that the storm would continue.

In mid-afternoon, we had our first a call to general quarters. The single hatch was closed and I sat praying that this was not the time. Several of us moved closer to the stretcher cases. We had promised that we would do all in our power to save them in the event of an attack. I had to avert my eyes several times at the sight of the panic registered on their faces.

Night came and we tried to sleep. The ship was a madhouse. It rolled and pitched, making the dysentery patients retch. An Englishman, delirious from a high fever caused by malaria, persisted in yelling, "General Wavell! General Wavell!" all night long, while Gordon and I restrained him to prevent him from trying to leave the ship. He insisted that the general had sent for him and he was determined to follow orders. There was no room in the small hold for a rampaging patient; there were too many ways that he could have hurt himself.

The ship continued on its way. The storm subsided and the hot tropical sun soon forced us to take off our woolen uniforms. The stench from stale perspiration, emesis, raw rubber and incontinent stretcher cases was beyond description. I felt that we must all suffocate, and soon.

During the first seven days at sea, general quarters was sounded every few hours. We sat, petrified, each time, scarcely daring to breathe and praying silently.

On the afternoon of the tenth day, general quarters was sounded again. We began to pray. There was a sudden, rending crash, followed by a dull thud that shook the *Awa Maru* much as a dog shakes a kitten. The ship bucked violently, rolled and bucked again. We moved closer to the stretcher cases, trying to impart to them a courage that we did not feel ourselves. The less said about the way we felt the better. We were all sure that the tiny tin tub was going to the bottom. No one spoke, not even the guards. After what seemed like ages, an all-clear was sounded and we learned from the guards that the skipper felt sure a torpedo had struck the propeller screws. Other than this, the ship was undamaged.

The next morning, the chattering of the guards made us realize that something quite momentous was taking place above decks. In a few minutes, a guard explained that we were coming into the harbor at Moji, Japan, on the northeastern tip of Kyushu. Our pleasure at having survived the trip was enormous, but suddenly we began to ask each other how we would be treated now that the Japs would have us on their home soil. To say that we were apprehensive was the understatement of the war.

We remained on board that night and, the following morning, were marched through swirling snow to a parade ground, in front of a barn-like assembly building. All of us were lined up for an interminable *tenko*. This included the stretcher cases; the dysentery patients lay hiccupping with snow and wind lashing into their gaunt faces. We could not restrain angry tears of frustration and pity, but were powerless to remedy the situation.

It was almost dark when the *tenkos* were finished and we were herded into the huge, icy hall. We were stiff from the long hours at attention in the cold, but there were only two tiny stoves to heat the large structure, one at either end. The only difference in being inside and out was that inside no snow fell in our faces and some of the wind was cut off.

We placed the stretcher cases around the small fires and bribed one of the guards to bring them some hot tea. Their faces were blue from the cold and they were shaking with hard chills. The guard took the money, but no tea ever came.

Later, we were served a small quantity of what looked like garbage: cold rice, cold cabbage, cold seaweed, and an icy pickle. Chuck, Marv, Gordon, Bob, Tex and I settled in a corner close together, trying desperately to get warm. Our teeth chattered non-stop; three years in the tropics had not prepared us for the cold weather. It was quite dark outside.

Suddenly, I heard a hissing sound. Looking behind me, I saw a tiny Jap soldier. He held a packet of cigarettes in his right hand and the forefinger of his left hand to his lips. He dropped the packet into my lap. He was obviously afraid that the guards would catch him. All of us nodded our thanks and moved our lips soundlessly. He smiled and disappeared as quickly as he had come.

We settled down on the bare floor with our half-rug over us, to try to get some sleep. The rugs were not large enough to cover our bodies and we woke continually throughout the night to shift them from one part to another of our half-frozen anatomies. Near dawn we gave up.

After breakfast, which was an exact replica of the dinner of the previous night and equally cold, we were again marched through town, this time to the railway station. The black-tiled roofs of Moji were all but hidden by the snow.

Along the way, we passed women and very old men shoveling snow or collecting garbage. Some of the women were pregnant and others had small babies strapped to their backs. The day was bitterly cold and they stopped at intervals to warm their hands at small fires kept burning in pails. The expressions on their faces were a combination of resignation and despair. I could not imagine American women doing this kind of work, even in time of war.

At the station 150 of us, with gear and including stretcher cases, were jammed into one railroad car. The guards warned us no to try to see through the slatted blinds covering the windows. The shade on my side, however, had a hole in it and I relayed anything I felt might be of interest to the others.

We traveled through mountainous country, not unlike parts of the Blue Ridge Mountains, the difference being an occasional glimpse of the sea. At the small village where we stopped briefly, loudspeakers were blaring the war news, announcing the rationed commodities, or notifying the villagers what items were deleted from the list of available goods.

The railway stations teemed with Japanese people, mostly women and children. The former wore pajamas with tight waists, shawls, or towels wrapped about their heads and clogs, sneakers or sacks on their feet. Small children wore every kind of clothing imaginable, including pieces of Jap uniforms and kimonos of varying description. They were all barefoot, although it was still snowing heavily.

We slept in our seats and, when I awakened, guards were yelling, "Speed-o! Speed-o!" and morning had arrived. They told us that we had arrived at our destination. We were herded outside where a tiny village, heavily blanketed with snow, clung to a low range of hills. It was obvious from the 55-foot-high piles of dross and slag that it was a coal-mining village.

Our reception committee was decidedly hostile. As we started on our trek toward the village, Jap civilians of all ages surged about us jeering, cursing us and throwing stones. We didn't need a Japanese-American dictionary to tell us the meaning of Jap curses. We had had ample experience with them in the past three years.

A halt was called before several tired-looking Japanese men, who later proved to be coal-mining officials. We stood in the snow once more for more than an hour while each guard and each mining official took a separate *tenko* and disagreed about the number. Finally, we were told to march.

At least half of our reception committee followed us, still jeering and throwing stones. Their faces registered indifference, as though they were automatons following the direction of some unseen commander, but, actually, their hearts were not in the work. The children were clad in a motley assortment of filthy rags and the kimonos of the women were dirty and wrinkled. The adults wore clogs, but the young were barefoot and every child had a seeping nose and bellies bloated from malnutrition.

I saw Chuck looking at a small boy of about seven and tears rolled unchecked down his heavily lined face, which still wore a heavy coat of jungle tan. No doubt the small boy was near the same age as his small son, Peter.

The new camp was enclosed by a high wooden fence. The buildings were wooden huts; ten men were assigned to each room. We were issued five paper blankets, a work uniform and were treated to a speech.

The guard who instructed us told us that we were to work in the coal mines, that our camp was called Number 24, that it was only one of many in the area. The other POWs were doing work around the wharves and in the industrial area. We were, he said, to be given two weeks of exercise because of our skinny physiques. Should we attempt an escape, we would be shot.

Following the speech, we were allowed to eat. Breakfast consisted of hot water with a few minnows floating around in it. Bob called it "scrap of desolation stew," and it was all I could do to thwart an impulse to throw it back into the face of the guard who gave it to us.

Gordon, always sensitive to any mood change in any of us, asked me what was wrong. "You look like you're about to slip your trolley," he said.

I proceeded to tell him, "I've just had one too many Jap speeches, Gordon. They all say the same thing, but what they don't say is more important. We'll work, they say, but what they mean is, we'll work and starve and maybe be killed in a lousy Jap coal mine. From what I've seen of it, I have not been impressed with their technical prowess. The mines can't avoid being dangerous. We'll not survive this, period. My mother will tell people she had an older son, but he was killed in the war, or died as a POW. No one knows for sure which.

"Everyone will feel sorry for her. My father will refuse to talk about it at all. My sisters and brother will remember my death as the first real sadness of their lives, but they will forget, eventually."

"Hey, Jim! Cut it out, or we'll all be crying in our damn stew!" McCann shouted, abruptly.

"I think I know what set you off, Jim,' Gordon began, as I paused for breath. "The jeers of those civilians got under your skin. I know how you feel. It gets you; it's one thing for a man to dish it out with a rifle butt when he's your enemy, but when women and little kids throw stones at you …"

He was right. My feeling toward the civilians was not one of enmity; certainly I wished them no harm. I wanted to go home and have an end to this miserable war. I had not started it. I wished no one harm. I wanted an opportunity to finish my education and make my mark in life.

We finished our stew, went into our cubicles and wrapped ourselves in the paper blankets. My teeth chattered endlessly and I couldn't recall having been as cold in my life. No one spoke for a few minutes, then Bob's head shot out of the blankets in which he had wrapped himself, mummy-style. His blue eyes sparkled with amusement and his snub nose wrinkled in a grin.

"I have something to tell you. It'll make you laugh. Maybe you could use a good laugh. I meant to tell you before, but it slipped my mind. No doubt my subconscious made me wait for the right moment. Well, the last day we were in Singapore, Morgan came to me and told me how much he appreciated what we had done for him in the jungle. He said we had saved his life."

"We did?" I asked, incredulously. "I don't recall having saved his life. I remember wishing he had died before he got into the Texas National Guard. That's a fine outfit and it doesn't deserve to have a fellow like Morgan in it."

"I remember planning to push him in the river when the rains made it high enough," mused Tex, "but it got so danged muddy and I was busy carryin' water and diggin' graves and it plum slipped my mind." Tex's handsome, dark face took on an expression of genuine regret.

Bob went on with his story. "Well, he said we saved his life the night we got the quinine for him from the Chinese cooks. You know, the night he thought his family was in the tree?"

"I hope you told him we only did it to stop his caterwauling, so's we could get some sleep," said Marv.

A look of annoyance crossed Bob's face. "Oh, you bunch of cheap cynics!" he said, in disgust. "The guy was really shook and I mean shook-un-strung-upset. Anyway, he was really moved. He said that was the first time in his life anyone had ever done him a favor and refused pay for it."

"Who refused pay for it?" demanded Chuck, indignantly. "Them G ... D ... quinine pills cost *five dollars apiece*! And let me tell you something else! Mike Sullivan would be alive today, if that skunk Morgan hadn't taken such a big cut when he got the food for us from the bungs." Chuck sat up on his bunk and shook his finger at Bob. "He's in the same class with them thieving black market Japs. He'd steal the pennies off a corpse's eyeballs."

"Nope. Not any more he wouldn't. I tell you, he's a changed man," Bob insisted.

"A skunk don't change his scent. Leastwise, I never knew one that did," drawled Tex.

"You go right ahead and think he's changed, but I wouldn't trust him with *my* wife, *my* money, or even *my* old baggy mother-in-law," snorted Chuck. "By the way, where is he now? You don't s'pose he's been left behind for good?" he asked with a hopeful grin.

We looked at each other and, suddenly, the tiny room seemed to brighten.

"By golly, it's some kind of omen!" exclaimed Marv.

"Could be, could be," Bob agreed.

We felt that if we had finally shaken our particular nemesis, things must be looking up.

"This is one time I'll try positive thinking with a vengeance," I told them. "Morgan will not show up in Japan!"

"You know, it's funny about him," Gordon said, thoughtfully. "He made out better than we did for the first year of this POW bit. He got everything he wanted by cheating and double dealing, but in the jungle, when the going got rough, he had no inner fortitude to help him fight his own battle against starvation, bad treatment and disease. If he ever did a charitable thing for anyone, no one ever caught him at it. He never went near the sick. He was completely selfish—kinda like a child."

"I'm glad he's changed, if he has," I said, "but, the guards say all POWs will be shot if Japan loses the war. Even without him, where does that leave us?"

I hated to express this morbid thought, but I had tried for too long to be cheerful.

At the end of our period of rehabilitation we were taken into the mines. I knew as much about coal-mining as I knew about yak culture (or the care and feeding of gnus) but my knowledge and opinions were not considered to be of importance to Jocko, the guard who gave us final instructions and a head lamp.

"No stand up in car! No sing! No whistles!" he warned, his black eyes stern.

I thought, as we climbed into the small cable car, that I had never felt less like singing or whistling in my life. The morale of the whole group was as low as it had ever been in the jungles of Burma. Part of our depression could be attributed to the fact that we had seen two badly crushed Korean miners carried from the mine just two days previous to this.

The main tunnel was ten feet high. A stream ran through it, carrying seepage to the pumps. The tunnel grew narrower as we descended, culminating in a space large enough for a car and one man (assuming a man could twist himself into a pretzel).

I looked at the cracked timber braces across the top of the tunnel. They sagged, moaning ominously as bits of dirt fell, changing the stress on their burdensome load. Water dripped ceaselessly. I decided that I would rather be outside. I turned to look at the guard, but his gun seemed to restore my interest in mining. Should the tunnel cave in they would not even need to bury us.

Jocko pointed to a side tunnel about three feet high and delegated Bob, Gordon and me to pick the vein. Before leaving us he told us that we had been assigned to the most dangerous section of the mine. The coal dust was thick, making breathing almost impossible. If we turned to find a pocket of fresh air we came face to face with the opposite side of the tunnel and more coal dust.

We worked flat on our stomachs. When we could no longer endure the feeling of claustrophobia, unaided by the bad air, we moved out for a few minutes. Each man took turns moving into the narrowest section, replacing the man in trouble. We suffered from a choking sensation caused by the close quarters, the coal dust and a great sense of danger that never left us. Yes, we were greenhorn miners, but any fool could see that a major cave-in was imminent.

Two days after we began, while the Koreans were on shift, the cave-in came. We helped carry the miners out: men with broken backs, broken limbs and those who had been crushed to a bloody pulp. We said little, but all of us thought, "There, but for the grace of God ..."

The civilian guards insisted that we work as fast as possible. One of these we dubbed "Many-many," because he was constantly insisting that we did many-many feet of coal, fill many-many cars, or put up many-many braces. He was forced to give most of his instructions by gesticulation, since his total English vocabulary consisted of three phrases: "many-many," "boy-boy" and "OK"

After several cave-ins of less consequence we were finishing one evening and Bob asked the question that all of us had been avoiding, although it was uppermost in our minds: "When will the next big one come?"

"Tomorrow or the next day," predicted Tex.

"Forget about it," Gordon calmly advised.

"How can we forget about it?" Marv asked, angrily. "It gripes me that we went through the jungle working on the railroad and they couldn't starve us to death, then the hell ships and now they plan to maim or kill us in a lousy coal mine."

Gordon seemed imperturbable. "You're not going to die in a Jap coal mine, so keep your blood pressure down, Marv. Don't borrow trouble."

No one answered this, because we all felt we *had* trouble and were just being realistic.

"What kept you from being killed before this?" Gordon asked in the silence.

"Our friends ... teamwork ... a good constitution ... and luck," I told him.

"Partly luck," Chuck threw in. "With me, I hated the Japs too much to die. I gotta get back at them bastards—and I won't die until I've done it."

"Well," said Tex," Gordon wants us to say God was watchin' over us. He might be takin' care of the generals, but the privates and the low rank guys ... there's just too many of 'em. He might want to, but how could he?"

Gordon looked annoyed. "I'm not going to preach to you fellows. I know all of you believe in God, but you think it's sissy to come right out and admit it. Actually, it's sissy *not* to admit it. The Bible says every hair on your head is numbered and not a sparrow falls that God doesn't take note of it. Now, you're a farmer's son, Tex and you know how many sparrows you have just on your ranch. I'm not worried about any of you and I'm not worried about myself."

"You're the lucky one," Tex told him. "If we stick around you we'll make it, but if something happens to you, Gordon, I'm gettin' ready to talk to Saint Peter or Gabriel, or whoever has the shift when the time comes."

We continued to do our daily stint in the mines. The Japanese coal miners who worked with us seemed quite indifferent to the day-to-day progress of the war, while the guards showed intense interest in the smallest event. They discussed it constantly. Not realizing how much Japanese we had picked up during our long incarceration, they often gave us news which they should have kept from us. In this way we learned that Saipan had been taken, that our navy was near and that there were frequent devastating bombings of the home islands.

Occasionally, the guards heard us discussing these things and tried to minimize their importance. They boasted of their enormous air force and their formidable fleet and army. They boasted of the mighty Japanese Empire that, they declared, grew daily and of the Emperor, who not only was the greatest head of a government who had ever lived, but who had soldiers, sailors and pilots of unparalleled bravery.

"*Japan kaksan, bungo echi!*" (Japan great, number one!) declared Many-many. "*Amelican squoshi, dommi-dommi!*" (America small, insignificant, no good!)

Jocko repeated the same sentence time after time, "Sab Flancisco go *boom! Boom! Boom!*"

"How many times have they blown up San Francisco? Must be at least a million, according to their own accounts," I told Gordon.

We knew the Allies were winning the war; therefore, their remarks no longer angered us. We did, however, find them tiresome.

The Japs dynamited the mines every day. Instead of running, they stood back and *let her blow*. We were determined not to run if the little Nips did not, but, many times, I thought my head would surely be blown off.

Fear was always with us. Sometimes, while working, small stones and earth started falling in a steady cascade. When this grew to an ominous stream we lay on our stomachs in the tiny side tunnels, wondering when and which way to run. We prayed. Amazingly, we had worked for almost a month before a disastrous cave-in occurred. We had just gone off shift and no one was in the tunnel at the time. Timbers crumpled like matchsticks beneath the tons of rock and debris that blanketed machinery and cable cars. It took two shifts of men to tunnel a space large enough to retrieve the buried equipment.

We were shaken by this occurrence. We felt the clock ticking until it was our turn. It was impossible that we would be able to escape forever.

The tropical ulcers on my legs had become extremely troublesome, as had those of many of the others. We were taken out of the mines for a while and given what was called "light duty." We gardened on top of a mountain where our "light duty" consisted of breaking rocks with a pick and digging grass out of frozen ground.

Three days after I became a gardener another cave-in occurred. All of our men had been shifted to the main tunnel to put up braces and a group of Koreans had been relegated to duty in the side tunnels. The new cave-in was in the exact spot where I usually worked. I began to feel that I had a monopoly on narrow escapes.

On the following day, a B-29 flew over the camp, a painted silver plane against a painted blue sky. It was part of a bombing raid on factories at Kyushu, some of which were badly damaged. The sight of it brought freedom very near ... for a few minutes, at least. The guards bashed us, yelled and cursed while it was overhead. Later, it was discussed by them as a blow below the belt and just what could be expected from those unspeakably decadent Amelicans.

The next day I went back to the mines on the night shift. The B-29s began regular raids. The older guards began to change their outlook about the war. They confessed, after seeing the first of the massive planes, that it would take their country a little longer to win against such aircraft.

The old miners became quite congenial. They actually talked with us and told us daily that, "Pretty soon, you go momma, poppa home." This talk, coming from the Japanese, didn't sound right, but it gave us a tremendous morale boost. We began to feel sorry for these old men, who had known nothing but hardship and faced the same prospect well into the future (assuming they survived their miserable coal-mining system).

April passed and the raids continued. Our physical condition was deteriorating at a rapid pace. We had beriberi, pellagra, bad teeth, tropical ulcers and severe colds. On top of that we were literally starving to death. What food we were given was expended in doing the day's work and nothing was left to pad our skeletal frames. Our cheeks were hollow with deep, dark rings under our eyes; we often wondered how we could get through a day's toil.

Even the Japs were worried about us. They needed coal miners. Since their remedy for everything was exercise, Jocko told John that we were terribly scrawny and must have a sports day to fix us up. John told Jocko that the prisoners were starving to death and must have food before they could exercise. Jocko replied that that certainly sounded like an Amelican. How, he asked, could we have more food when our own navy was keeping all the supply ships away with their blockade and blowing up every fishing boat that put to sea?

Sports Day was instituted. One day each week we were forced to get outside and perform ridiculous antics in snow, rain and mud. This exhausted us and made us furious. A favorite "exercise" was to make us get down on hands and knees in the mud and snow and gallop. Another was to hop around on swollen legs in the cold; another was to chase each other around the enclosure. The absurd shenanigans reminded us of Naito; however, these guards were sober.

The Japs at Camp 24 had a peculiar system of diagnosis. If a prisoner could get out of his bunk, he was well; if he could not, he was sick and two fellow prisoners must carry him to the hospital where he was given no medication, no dressings and no treatment. His food allowance was cut because he was not producing. As soon as he could walk to the detail, he was put on light duty. Before he had actually recovered enough to do light duty takes he was returned to the mines. The only advantage of the hospital was bed rest, but its great disadvantage was the short rations. It behooved us to be up and about as soon as possible. If we recovered it was not because of medical care.

Gordon had held up well in the jungle. He had been ill less than most of us. When he did become ill he contracted everything offered in the way of maladies. He developed appendicitis, although it was not the most propitious time or place to have this disease. To make things more interesting, he also had the usual malnutrition and beriberi, and, added to these were dysentery, dental disease and exhaustion. He was bedridden for two months. During this time we prayed unusually earnest prayers for him.

The Jap in charge of the camp didn't share the warm feeling for Gordon that the rest of us had and daily grew more impatient to have him vacate his bunk and return to duty. Because of the delay in his return to the mines and the great impatience of the Japs he was ordered into the mines as soon as he could walk.

Since we had no dentist for the greater part of our time in prison camp—and when we had one in the jungle he had no instruments—we were our own dentists. When an extraction was necessary we used hammers, chisels and any other implement that might have the two features of being available and looking like it might do the job. Needless to say, the tooth broke off, the jaw became infected and the patient suffered acutely, post-surgically. It was not uncommon to see a number of POWs walking about the camp, their swollen jaws wrapped in a piece of calico, a native sarong, a scarf or an old piece of shirt.

In this camp we had an American doctor who said that two of Gordon's teeth must come out if he were returning to heavy duty. He promised to relieve us of the extractions. We were delighted, since Gordon had suffered particularly with these teeth.

A Jap doctor and a first-aid sergeant assisted with the operation. The only instrument available in camp was one pair of dental forceps. Consequently, the crown of the first tooth broke off at once. A guard was sent to the civilian hospital to obtain more instruments as quickly as possible. When these arrived the teeth were removed, piece by piece, with a dental chisel and no anesthetic. The whole bloody procedure took three hours and was acute torture for Gordon. We had always admired his stoicism, but this topped all previous performances.

He was put to bed because of excessive loss of blood, but, two days later, the Japs ordered him back to heavy duty in the mines. This was the sheerest folly and we were outraged. Gordon could not stand up without tottering, but was discharged from the hospital as cured. Two of us helped him to the wooden barracks we called home and onto his bunk.

On the following morning he was ordered to fall in with the rest of us for *tenko*. We marveled at his ability to stand up and wondered how long he would be able to follow orders. He received his headlamp with the rest of us. I had been put back on day shift. We walked to the mine slowly because of Gordon and started to board the cable car. Gordon raised his right foot, but that was as far as he got before keeling over backwards. He was unconscious.

Bob and I obtained a stretcher from the workshop and carried him back to his bunk. Chuck, who was on light duty about the camp, told us that the whole picture looked very weird from where he was standing. "The sun was just coming us," he told us later, "and, as it came over the mountain, you guys were all shown up against the sky It looked to me like two skeletons carrying a third one with an armed guard in the background. I was sure we'd had a cave-in and one of our guys was killed."

As far as my own feelings were concerned, all the hatred I had stored up for the Japs during almost three and a half years came boiling to the surface. Although in my present physical condition I could scarcely have punched my way out of a paper bag, I wanted to put the stretcher down and punch every Jap in camp in the nose.

I would have been incensed had any human being been treated as they were treating Gordon—even a Jap—but Gordon was my best friend, a man who never complained, who had sacrificed sleep, energy and money when he could not afford any of them for the sake of his buddies, time after time, a man too dedicated to our common cause to seek special consideration for himself, even when he desperately needed it. This was just too much.

The American doctor who examined Gordon told us that he had collapsed from loss of blood and exhaustion. We returned to the mines. The Japs, feeling the 20-minute delay occasioned by Gordon's collapse was too much time lost, had already sent a load of Koreans in our place. We waited at the mouth of the mine for the cable car to return for us.

We continued to wait, furious at the Japs, busy with our own thoughts. We waited: the car seemed to be taking an unusually long time. After several more minutes it still did not return.

"Look!" John exclaimed, excitedly. "The cable isn't moving."

The cable had indeed stopped and we realized something had gone wrong deep in the mine. We immediately began to walk into the shaft and, after a short distance, we discovered that there had been a tremendous cave-in.

Coming upon men and equipment half-buried in earth, timbers and coal, we began at once to attempt rescue work. When we were finished, there were five corpses and many crushed and mangled men, all Korean. We were stunned. Had Gordon not collapsed, we, not the Koreans, would have been riding the car. The narrowness of this escape left us shaky for days and inclined to believe that the Lord took care of His own where Gordon was concerned.

CHAPTER 16

"You Must Learn to Run!"

Allied planes continued to bomb Japanese cities but, near the end of May, we had a thrill that rejuvenated our lagging spirits. American bombers and fighters appeared over Sasebo, a naval base only 30 miles away. Air raid sirens wailed night and day for long intervals, bombers began to appear, rain or shine, and we worried about our camp being bombed. The Japs were extremely depressed and irritable. In the first week of August Sasebo was heavily bombed.

One day we had finished our shift in the mines and were walking back to our huts. The Jap guards looked at us strangely. Their faces were drawn and lined and some peculiar form of hysteria seemed to have seized them. They ordered us to roll our gear and practice running to the air-raid shelter. All of us had expected a raid for some time, but that did not explain the behavior of the guards.

Finally John and I could stand it no longer and went to find Jocko to get an explanation. When he was located he, too, behaved strangely. He looked at us oddly, refusing to talk. The muscles in his jaw kept working up and down.

At our insistence he finally broke his silence. "You must learn to run! You must run faster than you have ever run in your whole life!" he told us, obviously under a great emotional strain. He was adamant about keeping his knowledge a secret despite our pleadings. We could get nothing further from him.

We speculated about every conceivable happening from an imminent landing to heavy bombing raids on Tokyo.

"Maybe they've just gone nuts," suggested Chuck. "They wouldn't have far to go, you know."

"More than likely they took too much dope. These Japs are always hopped up on something even if it's only their hind legs," Tex suggested.

The mystery remained and on the following day when we came out of the mines they ordered us to practice running. Back and forth, back and forth from barracks to shelter—from shelter to barracks—we were forced to run.

When we were allowed to pause for breath, Bob, looking serious, gave us his opinion. "It would have to be a cataclysm to make those birds show an interest in our welfare. It has to be something monumental. We've seen them scared before, but they never took the least interest in whether we lived or died. They're scared of the Allies; they're afraid not to protect us, hoping we can protect them. But, the question is, from what?"

"Maybe the war has ended," Marv said, hopefully.

"Let's ask Jocko what's going on and insist that he tell us," I suggested. Gordon agreed.

We found him and insisted that he explain their strange attitude. He spoke English far better than most of the guards.

"Do you lika live?" he asked. "If you like life, you must run. Your people have made bomb which they drop from parachute. It is small and shaped like box. It kills hundreds ... thousands people. It take away city in one blast. You must run fast and do as we say or you be killed!"

This explanation left us as puzzled as before. The Japs always exaggerated and a bomb that wiped out a city sounded about as plausible as their stories of their pilots killing Allied pilots with rice cakes. That they were frightened was a certainty—and that could only be good news for the Allies. Our morale soared.

It was several days later that we heard a low, rumbling sound, followed by an explosion of a terrific magnitude. It sounded as though the whole world was being blown apart at its axis. A heavy roar came immediately after, much like hundreds of heavy guns being fired at a distance. The guards went completely berserk, shrieking and yelling and dashing about like madmen.

"The Allied invasion!" announced John, happily. "They're softening up the shoreline."

Since the noise seemed a great distance away, we felt it posed no great threat for us and waited happily for the Nips to regain their composure. When they finally came out of the shelter they told us that another bomb had been dropped. One of the huge ones. We did not believe them.

The Japs continued to act strangely. They looked at us with a kind of awe tinged with fear. They were too frightened to bash us, or even to threaten us. Something had, indeed, happened—but what?

On August 16, when we fell out for *tenko* in the early morning, Jocko told us that we would not work in the mine that day. "Something happen to stop work today. Maybe not go to work anymore."

We thought something of importance had happened and knew that the Allies were not too far away from Japan. Our first thought, however, was: Where are they sending us now?

When I asked this question of the other POWs, we all agreed that, outside of Africa and Siberia, there were not too many places we had not been.

We asked Jocko if we were having a holiday. He kicked at the dust and said we might not go back to work.

"They're gettin' ready to shoot us!" Tex said with finality.

We spent several hours concocting all the reasons why there was a stoppage of work. A transfer to some other Japanese island seemed the most likely. At 1 p.m. Jocko appeared again and told us to stand by for a general parade at 4 p.m.

At the designated time, we marched to the mess hall where the Japanese C.O., Major Yamaguchi, had ordered us to appear. He stood waiting, looking distraught about something; his usual air of arrogant superiority had given way to one of extreme dejection. His eyes were moist and he choked repeatedly, trying to deliver a speech. We didn't care how he said it; in fact, we heard nothing after the first sentence; the blood pounding in our ears drowned out part of the message. The speech, a copy of which we obtained later, was as follows: "The order has been given to stop the fight. You are to remain in this camp for this time and we should wait for further instructions. In the future, as well as before, the camp commandant will take responsibility for your rest, food and clothing and the necessary means of security. Each prisoner is expected to carry on his daily life as before."

Yamaguchi finished his speech and for a few seconds we stood, dazed. We had waited so long to hear these words that we were in a state of shock, of disbelief. Then the reaction came. Almost to a man we burst into tears. We turned and ran outside, into the bright sunshine.

"We are free!" we shouted. "We are free! The war is over!

Only a few weeks before, the guards had been boasting about what terms the Japanese would accept when they took over the White House! Now, we were free! We lost the next few moments in back-slapping, noisy laughter and shrieks of sheer delight; then we emitted a mighty whoop in unison and ran toward the kitchen. We all but dismantled it completely, to find every crumb available.

When the kitchen looked like Old Mother Hubbard's, we counted out our precious hoards of money and, since the gates were still locked boosted each other over the fence.

The Japanese civilians who had stoned us months before looked at us in fear and either ran or put up their arms to ward off blows. We explained as best we could that we wanted only food and were willing to pay for it. When they felt assured that we meant them no harm they took us into their homes, many refusing money for the food they gave us.

Throughout the next few days we roamed the countryside, seeking food. If the war had ended, we were determined not to arrive at home in our present emaciated condition. The food we found was in every possible form: on the hoof, in cans, raw, cooked and of questionable derivation in some cases. Camp No. 24 took on the appearance of a livestock yard and every room in the wooden barracks was a pantry. We desperately needed food and medicine. We may not have found medicine but we had food!

Throughout the next few days we moved as though in a dream. It wasn't easy to become accustomed to the idea of freedom after three and one-half years of slavery under the Nips. The guards were still with us and they had guns but we paid them no heed. They could have been a group of boys playing at being soldiers; they were, in truth, a sad group of soldiers, totally unprepared for defeat. How could these white men win the war against descendants of the gods? They shook their heads and wiped their eyes and, as Tex put it, "We feel for them, but we just can't reach them."

American planes buzzed the camp daily. Our morale was high enough that no one could have raised it further, but when the planes came over, we burst into song. Sometimes "The Star-Spangled Banner," sometimes "America," or any one of the dozens of songs we loved best and had tried to sing in the past—having received resounding bashings for our efforts. Now, no one raised a hand to stop us. This really was freedom. The Japs appeared desperately afraid of reprisals and stayed out of our way and out of our sight as much as possible. They were not singing. Now that we had food we had to use caution. We were ravenous and our bony skeletons were in desperate need of padding, but we had to use care to avoid overeating. It was difficult to stop when we wanted so much to keep eating. When Tex and Chuck overate and ended up in the hospital, no one said a word.

"There's one thing I can't understand," Gordon told John Sayre.

"What's that?" John asked, innocently.

"How you can manage to cook such marvelous food now, when the stew you gave us for years tasted so wretched!"

Now that we had the luxury to notice, we were hypercritical of each other's appearance. We didn't want our families to see us in our present condition.

"They'd start another war," Bob declared. "What would your mother say about you, Jim?"

"She wouldn't even know who I was!"

"Well, she wouldn't even let you in the back door unless she saw your birthmark or something. You look like a scarecrow that someone forgot to stuff with straw. No self-respecting tramp in Texas would let you join his club." This tirade was from John.

"Well, you look like one of those muscle boys, before he took the course," I retorted.

"You know, Jim," said Tex, seriously (his stay in the hospital had only been of one night's duration), "if your girl got herself hitched in '42, right after the Houston sank, she's probably got three kids by now, don't you reckon?"

He was eating a two-inch-thick porterhouse steak and I asked him how he would like to wear it around his ears, instead of eating it. The others were still roaring with laughter from his jibe, but I was having a bit of trouble enjoying this humor. The thought of my girl, Alicia, being married to someone else was something I didn't want to think about, even in a joking way. I knew, of course, that it was quite possible. We had sent messages from Changi, but had no way of knowing whether or not they had arrived. We had planned to be married since that first day in Sunday School when I had pulled the long, blue streamers on her hat. She had been five. I refused to think about it.

We no longer doubted that the war had ended. We went into town and listened to radio broadcasts in a radio store in Sendryu. On August 22, Major Yamaguchi sent for us once more.

He wore full uniform on this occasion, complete with shiny, black boots. He was, however, still moist-eyed and stammered through a speech that had to be the hardest he had ever had to make. As he struggled with his emotions and made several false starts, the irrelevant thought went through my mind that the top of his head came almost exactly to Tex's belt buckle. He was a pathetic little man, but it was too soon for me to feel any sympathy for him. "This is a message from the commander of the Main Camp," he began:

> It is a pleasure to be able to inform you that we have received orders of our army about the stoppage of the fighting on August 18. Since you have been taken prisoners, you must have been suffering very much from pain and fatigue for those long years of prisoners' lives.
>
> I can well imagine how you are feeling yourselves—happy to meet the very big day when you can return home, reunited again with your very dear personals. I sincerely congratulate you on your pleasure and at the same time heartily share the sorrow with you for those who could not live to meet this glorious day. The staffs in the camps under my command have exerted themselves according to the laws to provide you with certain foods as much as they could. But it is a pity, indeed, that we could hardly do as we wished, because of terrible shortage of food and other reasons. How could we do it under these hardest circumstances, during the severest war we have ever had? I expect and believe that you will understand it quite well.
>
> I have heard that in one of your camps you presented Red Cross food packages and some of your personal belongings to the office staff and people in charge of

work parties; and, in some other camps, there was a kind offer of presents to those who got damaged by this war.

All these, understand, are to show your deep feelings of compassion and clear understanding of things which are characteristic to gentlemen's spirit and we all appreciate it with deepest emotion.

You are still staying in this camp until you receive orders to move and, finally, to get you on board at the nearest harbors. So, I expect you to live here as quietly as before, under the regulations of each camp, holding the feelings of pride and honor fastly in your minds. Also, taking care of your health, and await the day until you get back to your mother again.

This hypocritical speech of Yamaguchi, ostensibly prepared by his superior, could not disturb us. We were going home! We would think about Japan later.

We departed toward our huts in a state of hilarity. As we cleaned out our gear, we were euphoric. This departure from a Jap prison camp was for keeps. We had survived. I looked at my most treasured articles and burst into giggles. They consisted of an old piece of wire, used countless times in many ways, from holding my roll of possessions together to giving extra strength to a bamboo platform that threatened to collapse. There was a rice coffee pot, a pail used to make "coffee" out of toasted rice and water and the automobile hub cap: these had served as my mess kit and had been the envy of all my POW friends. There was the worn sarong which had served as everything from a bandage for a troublesome tooth to an extra wrapping for my feet during snowy Japanese nights. I piled the lot in a corner of the hut and threw them a farewell kiss. They had served me long and well. Perhaps the Japs could find some use for them now.

I sat down and wrote a letter to my mother and one to Alicia. When I had finished the unreality of the situation seemed to have dissipated and I began to feel once more that I was a marine, not a POW. Up to this point I had felt something like a character in a play: I had kept looking over my shoulder, figuratively at least, for the Nips to come back with their fists and rifle butts, announcing that the play had ended.

While we were waiting for orders to leave the camp, the local Japs took us on guided tours of the surrounding territory. They wined and dined us, took us to church and introduced us to the cultural aspects of their country that were available in the area. These were the same people who had stoned us eight months before. Finally, they introduced us to a female Japanese barber, who gave us the first real haircut we had had in over three years.

On August 29, the B-29s came over the camp. This was one of the most exciting days of my life. August 27 had been my birthday, but the day that followed was happier than all of my previous birthdays rolled into one. The planes, painted red, blue, green and many other colors, flew back and forth over the camp dropping parcels, drums and parachutes of all colors, settling in the camp and in the village of Sendryu. The Japs were astounded at this latest demonstration of American ingenuity. To be truthful, we were as surprised as they, but tried to conceal our astonishment.

There was food—even milk chocolate—and clothing, enough for all of us. Most important, there were drugs. John Sayre opened a parcel of drugs and sat down on the ground to stare at them in disbelief. Bottles, tubes and packets fell in a pile in his lap. "Just look!" he said, ecstatically spreading his fingers protectively about the small mountain in his lap. "Beautiful, snow-white aspirin tablets, hundreds of them, and mercurochrome!" He clutched a bottle of the antiseptic to his chest and hugged it like he would an old friend.

We knew how he felt, but we didn't waste time exulting over the medicines. Pants legs came up and treatment began on the tropical ulcers. Salve and bandages were applied and then we began on the pellagra sores, tinea, ringworm and assorted abrasions and rashes, some of which we had had for two years. Perhaps we were afraid that the Japs would take the medicines away from us and sell them on the black market, as they had done with the Red Cross parcels.

When we were all treated and bandaged—and John had stopped hugging his mercurochrome bottle long enough to use it—we gathered food, clothing and more medicine and went to the hospital. Standing about with moist eyes, we watched the incredulity on the faces of the patients as they dived into parcels and drums and packages.

"Gordon, how many, many lives could have been saved in the jungle with just a few of these items!" I exclaimed. "I have just passed my twenty-fourth birthday and, for the first time in my life I really know what *freedom* means."

On September 2, the Jap officers held a banquet. We killed our last beef and the Allied officers were invited to join the Japs in the broadcast of the surrender, which did not come through.

The Japs fell in, with their gear, in front of the guard house after the banquet, for inspection by the Allied officers. They turned over to us weapons, ammunition, and the keys for all the camp buildings. This was a momentous occasion to those of us who had dreamed about this moment and boasted about it to each other. We had longed to see Japan's invincible, as they termed it, "samurai" humiliated before us as we had been humiliated by them.

As we watched, the thought occurred to me that this submission to Allied officers was something that they had not anticipated. They had never before lost a war. The arrogance and pride of the samurai, which had sustained them during our years of misery, had deserted them completely. They stood, a group of thoroughly miserable, dejected, completely wretched soldiers, drinking the bitterest of all cups. I could almost see them asking themselves how this could be. Were they not *meant* to be conquerors? Had they not only been told that they would win the war because they were descendants of the gods and were invincible, but that white men would be their personal slaves from then on? In all of their teachings no one had bothered to teach them how to accept defeat with dignity.

Hundreds of times I had thought, as had my shipmates, that we would take reprisals when the war ended. We would pay them back in full measure for murdering our comrades, for stealing our food and medicine and selling them on the black market, for beating women and striking the sick, for sending our men to stand in the hot sun until they fell from lack of food and water, for throwing the officers in the cells and feeding them rice with salt caking it, for driving splinters under the fingernails of the men and for burning them with cigarettes.

Now that the time had come I could not find it in my heart to strike a blow. They were the product of a special environment, quite barbaric in many ways. I could not forgive them, not yet, at least, but I did feel pity for them. Surrender was a bitterly humiliating experience. Tears streamed down the faces they could no longer save; these proud samurai were now our guests. We were all God's creatures, but it seemed to me that many of the Japanese had not yet found that out.

Matsui, the interpreter, tried to make the speech, but, in his attempt, choked on the words, his voice breaking and tears coursing down his cheeks. Again I felt pity, realizing at the same time that they were victims of their own false pride.

After this tearful scene, Dr. Goodman, our buffer who had protected us from the Japs throughout our stay in Sendryu (as well as they would let him), gave his own speech. He had obtained a bottle of saki and, as it went the rounds, he said, "We are free!"

This speech could not be improved upon and we responded with a chorus of yells and cheers.

When we had calmed down again, he continued, "We are free to tear down the village if we wish. We may travel wherever we wish without cost to us. We are free men; but we must use discretion."

Another series of shouts went up. Then, standing very still, we said, very solemnly and with all our hearts, not a dry eye in the crowd: "Here's to the Stars and Stripes. May they wave forever!"

CHAPTER 17

Home

On September 14, we left for Nagasaki. We donated the remainder of our food to the people of Sendryu. Our departure from the town was quite different from our arrival. Many of the Japanese civilians came to the station to see us on our way. Their hostility had disappeared, or, if any last vestige remained, we had struck it a mortal blow by our donations and our efforts to be their friends.

Waving back at them in the strange circular motion they employed, we climbed aboard a train which carried ten of us to a car. On the previous trip there had been 150 of us to a car. We had many good meals behind us in the last few weeks. We were clean-shaven, bandaged and, best of all, we were homeward-bound.

As the train prepared to pull out of the station—Japanese trains are not inclined to stay in one place longer than needed—Tex looked at Chuck and suggested that the latter start beating up a few Japs, since we were en route home and the opportunity would soon be lost.

"Aw, shucks, Tex. Did it ever occur to you that I've been pestered enough by you and might like to be left alone? I could be practicing some first rate diplomacy for all you know."

Tex was not to be shut off quite that easily: "Well, I just thought I heard you say a few times in prison camp, like maybe a couple of million, that you'd wipe up the ground with a few of these little bandy-legged jerks. I know you could do so, too, 'cause I've seen you fight. So, get goin' son, time's a'wastin' and the Good Lord knows when you'll get back here." He shook a long, skinny forefinger at Chuck.

"It's not that I've changed my mind; it's just that I have more important things to do. Why, those poor little old kids. I kinda feel sorry for them. What the hell kinda chance do they have, anyway, with no food, no clothes and a buncha squirrelly relatives that get down on their knees every morning worshipping an emperor that got them into all this mess?" He started to say something profane, but stopped. It was remarkable how few obscenities he used these days.

"You're chicken. Admit it. A little food and it goes to your head instead of to that scrawny carcass where it oughta go."

"Maybe I'll come back and give 'em a workin' over some day, but seein' those little runny-nosed kids in the snow last winter kinda got me. Barefoot in the snow, mind you."

"One of them reminded me of your Peter," said Tex, grinning.

"Shaddup!" roared Chuck and got to his feet. The train started with a sudden lurch and Chuck regained his seat.

"Your son won't be a baby anymore," said Gordon. "He'll be pushing eight, won't he?"

Chuck nodded. His hair was completely white, which Gordon attributed to his negative emotions. He showed the ravages of Jap imprisonment to a greater degree than most of us, although all of us bore its marks.

Tex had deep lines in his face, as did all of us and there were streaks of white hair in his thick, formerly pitch-black thatch.

The food had arrived too late and Gordon's beriberi was very bad. Both legs were swollen like balloons, almost thirty inches around in places. It would be months before he could dispense with crutches. He had gone everywhere with us in Japan, although it required two of us to help him to his feet and two to assist him up and down stairs. Between exertions, it was necessary for him to rest frequently. Anyone except Gordon would have given up and stayed in camp, but, as usual, he minimized his own problems.

We were beginning to understand him now. He tried to ignore his handicap and we realized he had his own rewards. He had not tried to evade falling in for *tenko* on the morning following his teeth extractions, knowing that the effort could kill him. His insistence on going to work, even when quite unable, had innocently been responsible for saving our lives. The unexpected, seemingly miraculous, result of his brave attempt to keep doing his share must have been a magnificent reward in his eyes. Gordon had his Faith, a workable faith and a practical one—something toward which we could all strive.

Bob McCann had lost three toes from tropical ulcers, but, except for loss of weight and gray hairs, looked much the same. Marv Jones was almost blind from vitamin deficiency and we had to read the newspaper to him. I had a more or less constant backache, which the doctors said would probably remain with me for life. But we were all alive. We had taken everything the Japs had dished out and had survived. We were the lucky ones.

Many POWs had been permanently handicapped and left unfit for the life of a private citizen as a result of these years of physical and mental abuse. As for those who did not survive, it seemed to me that their needless, useless and for the most part, very painful deaths should be viewed as shocking injustice and utter tragedy.

As for the Japs themselves, we felt the vicious guards and prison officials deserved severe punishment, possibly the same treatment they had inflicted on us for years. Yet, now, it was obvious to me that, to people with the native arrogance of the Japanese, the ignominy of defeat was a crushing punishment. This represented a step forward in the progress of mankind from primitive savagery. It had given us a certain humility—a maturity—a realization that not everyone was blessed with the freedom and plenty we Americans took for granted.

I thought of the wide, green, lush fields of my father's ranch, the beautiful view from a particular hill. Space. Freedom. A complete freedom from want. In a horrible contrast I thought of the rocky, handkerchief-sized vegetable patches where the Japs struggled to make their crops thrive.

As the train approached Nagasaki, I was stunned by the picture of desolation that met my eyes. Where previously a large city had stood, there was now a mass of rubble, blackened trees, twisted steel and devastated buildings. The city had virtually disappeared with one bomb's explosion. It was incomprehensible that a single bomb could have wreaked this havoc. No wonder the guards, Many-many and Jocko, had been petrified with fear. Here and there, a few Japs, clad in rags, picked forlornly at the ruins. For many of them, everyone they loved had disappeared in one fiery blast. What, I asked myself, if this had happened to Dallas, Houston, New York, or San Francisco? This whole war demonstrated man's inhumanity to man. We had won the war with our technical prowess.

I had been told that the Japs still had an army of ten million men, many of them on the Chinese mainland, when peace came. They could not believe that a surrender had been arranged. The bomb had been the coup de grace. It had averted any further additions to the staggering loss of the young men of a generation.

Deceit and fanaticism had given them an advantage for a while: they had sunk our navy, partook in a war that had us fighting on two fronts and planned to help the Germans rule the world. Their megalomaniacal leaders had never considered defeat. The Japs were good soldiers. I felt sorry for them. Thousands of them had died because of the militarism that had started in the 1930s.

While we watched the terrible picture that passed us from our train windows in silence, feeling genuinely depressed because of the horrible devastation, we were suddenly thrown into a quite different and joyous mood.

Our own United States Navy Band was playing as the train pulled into the station. What appeared to be half of the Marine Corps, the Navy and the Red Cross swarmed upon us. All of them seemed to be offering congratulations at once. The band played, the flags waved and we tried valiantly to eat the sandwiches and doughnuts and to drink the hot coffee with which the Red Cross workers plied us, but we could not. I choked on a huge lump in my throat and found it quite impossible to swallow. The other POWs were suffering from the same problem.

We had arrived at the station at 2:30 p.m., and, in less than an hour, had been debugged and were going aboard the U.S.S. *Haven*. It was quite different from the ships in which we were accustomed to travel and the hell ships faded into the background. Even the *Houston* could not be as white and as clean as this spotless ship. The waxed decks shone and I hesitated to put my foot down. Not only this but the sheets on the bunks had to be the whitest in the world, not to mention the pillow, which I touched just to make sure it was really as soft as it looked.

Nurses and corpsmen gave us first call on their attention, deluging us with newspapers, magazines, food and anything else we could wish for that the *Haven* could possibly provide. They even provided us with a radio and no one got shot for using it.

On the following morning, I talked to Lieutenant Swier, one of the nurses in the office. She knew a family by the name of Gee and asked if I were related to them. I had not talked to a white woman for almost three years and it felt surprisingly awkward. She put me at ease at once, however, and my misgivings were soon dissipated.

That evening we saw a movie on board, *The Seven Crosses* with Spencer Tracy. On the following day we were thoroughly examined by the Navy doctors and I was told I needed food and rest, but should be in good condition in time. Corporal Vandergrift gave me a cap and emblems and, on the following day, most of us were sent to Okinawa where we were visited by the Red Cross and sent to the hospital at Guam.

Nine days later, we left Tex and Chuck at the hospital for more rest and treatment and, after planning a reunion in the States, we boarded the U.S.S. *Catron*, en route to San Francisco. We had regained a bit of our lost poundage and were, needless to say, desperately anxious to get home.

No words can describe my feelings as the ship swept under the Golden Gate Bridge and I saw San Flancisco, as Jocko called it, sprawled upon its seven hills. How many times had the Japs told us that it had gone "*boom-boom*, all gone, no more," but there it was, as though the Japs had never started a war. It looked good enough to eat, Marv told us, but only POWs thought of everything in terms of food.

We were taken to Oak Knoll Naval Hospital and promptly checked out on liberty. As soon as I could reach a phone, I put in a call for home. I had planned this conversation with my parents and Alicia for too long to remember, but, when my mother's soft drawl came over the wire, I found it impossible to say a word for several seconds.

She kept repeating, "Jimmy, darlin', are you there? This is Mama," yet I could not speak. As soon as I found my voice and began to talk she burst into tears and all I can say is that it was a very wet situation. I finally managed to convey that I was well and would be home as soon as the doctors would permit. She told me Alicia would meet me at the train. My knees sagged, my mouth felt dry and my heart pounded. How, I asked myself, would Alicia be meeting me at the train if she were married to someone else? Tex's teasing had been bothering me more than I cared to admit.

Bob McCann's aunt and uncle took the four of us—John, Marv, Gordon and me—for a tour of the Bay cities and we had our first wonderful stateside dinner in San Francisco I returned to the hospital to find a wire from Alicia. She would meet me in Dallas.

Three days later we were transferred to the U.S. Naval Hospital at Norman, Oklahoma and permitted to go home for a weekend.

The train pulled into the station at home, just as it had on many a Friday afternoon while I was in college. The whole town, including most of the babes in arms, had turned out to meet me. My only immediate problem was getting my mother, father, Ben, Alicia and my sisters all into two arms at once. This was not to mention the countless aunts, uncles and cousins who had joined the reception committee.

During my first postwar dinner at home, no one seemed to know whether to laugh or to cry. It was a memorable occasion for all of us and, while there was much laughter, it was occasionally choked off by tears. There was not the slightest doubt in any of our minds that we were the happiest people in the world to be together ... and to be free.

I spent the night in the bed that I had dreamed about too many times throughout the monsoon season, when we had sat huddled before a tiny fire while the wind shrilled through the apertures of the hut. The Texas autumn night was just cool enough to make the blankets feel right and, while I was thanking God for the miracle that had brought me back alive to this house, I fell asleep.

I awoke to the aroma of freshly baked bread and newly made coffee—and all of the marvelous scents and wonderful sounds that meant I was home.

It was months before I was discharged from the hospital where we had been sent to recover our equanimity, in Guantanamo Bay, Cuba. I had been promoted to sergeant. One of my first and most enjoyable tasks following this was to help remove my name from a memorial plaque in my home town which listed the names of men who had not survived World War II.

Marv and Tex were married within the year and are now Texas ranchers. Bob and Gordon are still bachelors. Bob is teaching in a West Coast university and Gordon is, of all things, an attorney.

After serious consideration and mutual agreement, Alicia and I decided to go our separate ways. I was married two years later to the daughter of an American diplomat in Havana, Cuba. No one needs to be told who the ushers were. John Sayre, whose voice had raised us from the deepest gloom in prison camp, sang at the wedding.

At the reception which followed at the U.S. Embassy in Havana, I was introduced to a statuesque blonde who turned out to be Chuck's wife, Gertrude. Chuck told us that she had lost a great deal of weight while working as a welder in an airplane factory near Los Angeles. He seemed quite pleased with her resultant beauty. They now have a chicken ranch near Santa Rosa, California, in the Valley of the Moon.

Epilogue

As I sat in my comfortable, secure home a quarter of a century later, I had every reason to be satisfied with my existence. Life had been good to me since the war. True, I didn't see much of my buddies anymore; they had gone their way and I had gone mine. I, in my late forties, now more logical and careful, looked back on my POW experience, my three and a half years as a "guest" of the samurai, as one of the natural hazards of war. Time is merciful. I no longer smelled the filth, saw the disease, or heard the terrible shrieks of crushed and dying men in my dreams. No longer did I relive the hunger or the smash of rifle butts against my skull. The Japanese were now our friends. Tokyo was the largest city in the world and Japanese industry sold most of its products in America.

I can no longer blame the Japanese for their brutality. The lower echelon, as well as their superiors were only following orders. The extreme cruelty of the guards was a reflection of the treatment accorded them by their own officers.

In earlier wars Japan had been very fortunate. She planned her wars well and one decisive battle sufficed to make her a victor. She expected the same result in World War II. Her pilots did not destroy the aviation gasoline when they bombed Pearl Harbor: they had been instructed that it would be used when they had secured the Hawaiian Islands. Midway was to be the scene of their next decisive battle, but the failure at Midway left their Japanese strategists floundering. Right up until the last weeks of the war, the Emperor was pleading for the one decisive battle that his officers were incapable of delivering; they had underestimated the magnitude of the foe.

America has been excoriated for dropping the atom bomb. No thinking person would deny that this was a terrible tragedy. Japanese scientists were busily creating an atom bomb of their own when ours fell, but few realize that the firebombing of Japan caused far greater damage and many more deaths than the atom bombs. The atom bombs that dropped on Nagasaki and Hiroshima ended the war at the cost of millions of lives, but they set Japan on a course of peace, away from militarism. The democratic process became the way of life in Japan. The Emperor's deification has ceased.

War is a senseless and barbaric pursuit. If we are to live in freedom we must fight back when attacked. But, as Abraham Lincoln put it, we did the best that we could but there will always be those who cannot agree with us and "ten angels swearing" will not convince them we were right.

I sat wondering at the ironies of war, encased in the pleasantries of the present. I wished that Chuck Satterlee and Marv and Johnny Sayre and the others could be with me now. Perhaps the memories would not be so dim with them. They were growing dimmer with each passing day for me. But, why, I asked myself, was I in this mood?

My wife tapped me lightly on the shoulder and handed me the morning paper. "Another cup of coffee, honey?" she asked.

"No, thanks," I answered and opened the paper to the front page, as she walked quietly from the room. She knew my mood. She knew that I would need to be alone.

A four-column picture stared at me from that front page. A barefooted, rag-covered Air Force lieutenant, his bandaged head seeping blood, had been caught by the camera being marched between two guards in North Vietnam. The caption beneath the picture said, simply, "Captive American."

Suddenly, before me there was a screen and some unknown, unseen projectionist was rewinding the film. Again, I saw the *Houston* in her death throes, smelled the filth and disease, felt the blows and hunger.

Forty thousand young Americans have been slaughtered so far in Vietnam* in the longest war in our history, with thousands permanently maimed and shattered for life. In North Vietnam there are POWs whose loved ones have not heard from them for years and have no knowledge

---

* The final tally would be 58,000.

of whether they are alive or dead. How many of these POWs are in the same age bracket that I was 25 years earlier? How many were going through the same hell?

Men—American men—have walked on the moon. It will not be long before American men will walk on Mars or Venus or some other far-distant planet. There seems no limit to how far we can go.

But have we gone so far, actually? War is everywhere. American is the greatest country in the world, certainly the most powerful and affluent. But is she fighting hard enough for peace? As our men explore space, what about the inequities right here on earth?

I wanted desperately to talk to Chuck Satterlee or Marv or Johnny Sayre, or maybe Tex or Gordon. I particularly wanted to hear Chuck's voice, his salty, irreverent remarks, right now. I reached for the phone to dial his number. Just at this moment, my wife returned with a second cup of coffee, so I pushed the phone away and smiled up at her.

She took the newspaper from my lap, folded it and laid it on the table. "The news is all sad," she said softly. "The coffee will take the chill off."

She left me to my thoughts once more. I looked toward the broad windows and out into the morning sunshine that was bathing the shrubs at the rear of the house and just then a funny thing happened.

Chuck was standing in the garden, beyond the window, but his voice came to me as clear as though he were right next to me in one of the Japanese POW camps.

"You wrote a book, pal," he was saying, "because you feel America needs your story right now more than ever. Congratulations! But don't end with the book. Keep the faith, Jim. And don't forget to pray. You and me's got faith—faith in God, faith in America—faith in that good ol' flag that waved to the last as the Houston went down."

Strange, but Chuck hadn't uttered a profane word—as he often did— when he and I were "guests" of the samurai.